IMAGES OF THE PAST
COALMINERS

Although not adopted in Britain, many Catholic countries refer to St Barbara as the patron saint of miners, her canonisation celebrated on 4 December. In Europe, workers will often place a statuette of St Barbara at the entrance of a tunnel during construction, as a safeguard against accidents. This bronze plaque representing St Barbara was commissioned for a hospital in north-east France, close to the German border, the saint surrounded by miners' cap-lamps and helmets. Notice the modern colliery in the background.

A sight once common on streets throughout Britain and Europe, a delivery man eases a sack of coal on to his back, bound for a local household. France, undated, c.1960s.

IMAGES OF THE PAST
COALMINERS

BRIAN ELLIOTT

Pen & Sword
HISTORY

First published in Great Britain in 2015 by
PEN AND SWORD HISTORY
an imprint of
Pen & Sword Books Ltd,
47 Church Street,
Barnsley,
South Yorkshire.
S70 2AS

A CIP record for this book is available from the British Library.

ISBN 978 1 84563 147 5

Typeset by Chic Graphics

Printed and bound in England
by CPI Group (UK) Ltd, Croydon, CR0 4YY

Pen & Sword Books Ltd incorporates the imprints of Pen & Sword Archaeology, Atlas,
Aviation, Battleground, Discovery, Family History, History, Maritime, Military, Naval, Politics,
Railways, Select, Social History, Transport, True Crime, and Claymore Press, Frontline
Books, Leo Cooper, Praetorian Press, Remember When, Seaforth Publishing and
Wharncliffe.

For a complete list of Pen & Sword titles please contact
Pen & Sword Books Limited
47 Church Street, Barnsley, South Yorkshire, S70 2AS, England
E-mail: enquiries@pen-and-sword.co.uk
Website: www.pen-and-sword.co.uk

Contents

This portrait-style photograph of a young miner wearing a large lamp attached to the front of his helmet, its battery out of sight, was used for promotional purposes by the cap lamp's manufacturer CEAG. Founded in Barnsley in 1912, this company became a national leader in the making of a variety of electronic lamps for the mining industry, employing over 800 people, mainly women, at his peak during the Second World War. Their 'Lumax' bulbs and lamps were also used in the developing motor, aircraft, maritime and scientific industries. For a detailed history see *Memories of Barnsley* magazine, Issue 24, 2012. CEAG Barnsley

Foreword

Every community is a product of what has gone on before – rooted in the people, places and events of the past, which extend their influence throughout generations. This is particularly true in the coalfield communities of Britain and Barnsley, where the industry dominated every facet of people's lives. To understand this is to understand so many challenges and, to that end, historical records are a vital educational tool, both for students and society as a whole.

History is not all about kings and queens, battles and births. It is also about recording the everyday – the working conditions, the food, the tools and clothes, the chores, the relationships. Yet those who appear in this montage of the everyday are often overlooked by history. Resources were scarce, priorities different. Which is why a book such as this one is rare treasure indeed. It brings together a fascinating array of images, capturing so much and provoking even more questions.

My thanks go to Brian Elliott, the author of this hard work, for collecting these images and for his insightful commentary. The history of coal mining may be etched upon our landscape but this book now also ensures it is better reflected in our history.

Dan Jarvis MBE MP
Barnsley Central

Introduction

The main purpose of this book is to pay tribute and give proper recognition to coalminers at a time when the once great coal industry of Britain has almost gone. As I write this there appears to be little prospect of UK Coal not fulfilling their plan to close Kellingley and Thoresby collieries. This leaves Hatfield Main near Doncaster as our only remaining deep mine. Within living memory, the contraction of the industry was most marked in the 1960s when the NCB under the chairmanship of Alfred (Lord) Robens closed 400 pits and about one job in every two disappeared. Traditionally mobile, many redundant miners still found jobs, albeit in more distant pits. Then the rapid run down in the wake of the 1984-85 miners' strike, despite the gallant efforts of movements such as Women Against Pit Closures, left very few pits able to continue into the 21st century.

The compilation of *Coalminers* also occurs at a very apt time in world history. Many thousands of miners and their families played their part in the global conflict that became known as the Great War, its centenary years now being commemorated. In 1914, the number of miners that responded to Kitchener's Call contributed to a significant reduction of manpower in the pits of Britain. I've included tributes to two former miners who served in the First World War: one a young 'forgotten' poet, a 'Sheffield Pal' who died on the Somme and a South Wales Borderers 'miner-VC' whose gallantry was extraordinary.

Patriotism apart, many pit lads enlisted thinking that the army was 'a better life', far less dangerous than work underground. This was understandable as well over a thousand men and boys were killed in the coal industry every year and at least five times more suffered injuries. The great tragedy of Senghedydd was fresh in the memory of many, especially in South Wales. This and other disasters demonstrated the human devastation that could still occur to pit communities anywhere 'in an instant'.

Although the limited scale and extent of an 'old images' book cannot pay full justice to my aim, I have tried to take great care in both the selection of illustrations and their captions. Ceri Thompson at Big Pit National Coal Museum (Museum of Wales) has always responded to my queries and questions; and help is much appreciated from Ellie Swinbank (National Mining Museum Scotland), Rosemary Preece (National Mining Museum for England) and their colleagues, though I hasten to add that any errors are entirely my own. Martin Freeth and the Freeth family

A miner 'testing for gas' is one of the most iconic images associated with the coalmining industry. This sculptural example has the additional symbolism of a hewer's pick and can be seen at the Woodhorn museum site at Ashington in Northumberland. The figure surmounts a tall column of stone that forms part of the memorial to the thirteen miners who lost their lives following an explosion in Woodhorn pit on 13 August 1916. This spectacular mining monument was originally placed at Hirst Park in 1923.

kindly gave permission for me to reproduce several images relating to their late father's (W.H. Freeth's) artwork and I am very grateful for their kindness. Thanks are also due to Stewart Williams (Publishers) of Barry for permission to reproduce several images from their excellent series of 'old photographs' books, in particular *Old Rhondda* and *Rhondda Remembered*; and to Andrew White for permission to use several images from the Irvin Harris Collection. The majority of images in Coalminers are from my own collection or camera, therefore remain with my copyright. Credits to any other known copyright holders are given at the end of captions.

For military advice and guidance thanks to Jayne Daley and Andrew Featherstone.

My thanks also go out to Dan Jarvis MBE MP for writing the foreword and to Lisa Hooson and her colleagues at Pen & Sword Books.

Chapter One

Portraits and Profiles

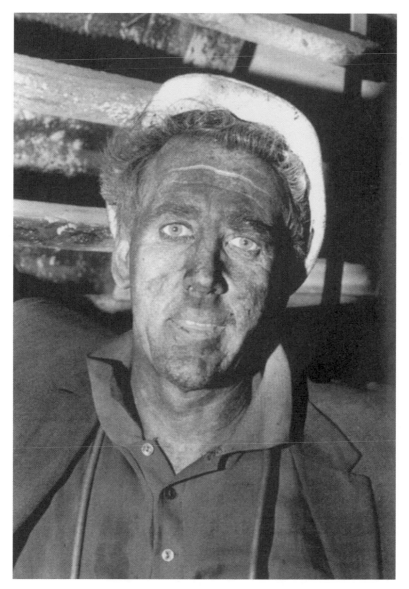

A fine close-up shot of the face chargeman at Creswell Colliery, Tom Hendley, in 1978. At times Cresswell (Derbyshire) was the scene of mass picketing in 1984 during the miners' strike and closed in 1991. *Sheffield Star*

Detail from 'The Collier', a plate (no.3) taken from George Walker's *Costume of Yorkshire*, originally published in 1814. The figure is a somewhat romantic image of a Middleton Colliery, near Leeds, miner, who is described as 'returning from his labours in his usual costume'. Smoking from a clay pipe, one hand on a walking stick and the other supporting a wicker basket, there's no sign of any muck or grime, the workman appearing like a farm labourer in his Sunday best. However, Walker does acknowledge that the collier's attire 'of white cloth bound with red, may probably be ridiculed as quite inconsistent with his sable occupation'; and qualifies his appearance due to 'frequent washing'.

John Evans who was buried without food or light, during the space of 12 days & nights, in a Coalpit at Minera, near Wrexam, 120 yards below the surface of the Earth, September 27th 1819.

One of the most remarkable survival and rescue stories in British mining history concerns a man called John Evans who worked at Pentrefron Colliery in the Wrexham area of north Wales. On 27 September 1819, the 120-yard deep mine was flooded and 3 of the 19 men working at the time were trapped underground. Two bodies were recovered by the searchers after 8 days but little hope remained of finding a third person alive. A coffin was prepared for his burial, its name plate inscribed. After 12 days explorers heard a voice calling to them, debris was cleared and John Evans was found sitting in the darkness. He had survived by eating candles and drinking water which had dripped down on him. Very weak but still able to walk, Evans was escorted out of the pit and taken home on a cart, accompanied by a large and triumphant crowd. Apparently Evans later made use of the makeshift coffin, converting it into a cupboard for his home. Understandably, he did not return to mining, passing away peacefully 47 years later, aged 75, a legendary figure captured for posterity in this old engraving. *Amgueddfa Cymru/National Museum Wales*

The Victorian magazine *The Graphic* was notable for its high quality illustrations, the work of very able artists. In the April 15 1876 issue a full-page engraving of 'The Miner' appears, described as number 6 of a 'Heads of the People' series. It is a superb image, the face of the veteran pitman captured by the light of his Davy lamp. His expression, certainly his eyes, seem somewhat sad and the artist has emphasised his large hands. Carrying a couple of picks over his left shoulder, it is also interesting to see that he is wearing a cloth cap, worn with the peak placed at the back of the head. He is also shown, perhaps unusually, sporting an ear ring. Whether captured from life or a composite sketch, it remains one of the most striking portraits of a Victorian miner.

In the early 1900s, the Clay Cross Company published a series of 25 picture postcards in order to promote their award-winning Derbyshire coal. Based on photographs that may have been taken a few years earlier, in the 1890s, most of them are very compelling images when viewed today. This portrait-style example shows George Alibone, who is described as a 'getter' (or hewer) of "C.X.C Gold Medal" Coal'. He worked at Clay Cross No.2 pit. George is seen in his work clothes – probably at the start of his shift – holding a flamed safety lamp and pick. Notice the cloth cap and clogs and his trousers are, typically, tied with string just below the knees. Although posed, it is one of the best underground photographs of an Edwardian miner.

Studio photographs of male miners displaying their tools or equipment are not common. This example of an unnamed miner, possibly from Durham, is taken from an early postcard, which dates from about 1910, though the original image may be several years older. Looking smart and carrying a gauzed flame safety lamp, he was probably an official, maybe a deputy or even a manager; and certainly proud of his status.

Carrying home his pick, lamp, snap and water tins, this posed but compelling image of a miner is also interesting because he is shown wearing his work clothes. Note the soft cap, which appears to have a badge attached – possibly denoting his membership of a miners' association (trade union) lodge or area. Believed to be from Lancashire, c.1900.

This pair of Scottish pit lads, cigarettes drooping from their mouths, appear facing the camera with a good deal of attitude, their demeanour further enhanced through an impressive array of tools. The long drills, used for hand-boring are certainly spectacular, alongside more commonly mine-associated items such as sharp-pointed hewers' picks. Attached to their jauntily-worn caps are tallow lamps and their black faces suggest that the image was taken not long after the end of shift. It is also interesting to note their 'nicky tams', trousers hitched up and held by string in the traditional manner. This kept the legging ends relatively dry in muddy conditions, though some sources suggest that the practice was to make sure that mice or rats could not ascend legs! Unknown names or date, but probably around 1900. *Scottish Mining Museum*

Sons and grandsons often followed fathers and grandfathers in the coalmining industry. This interesting group shows three generations of Scottish miners – the Gray family from Shieldhill (Gardrum pit) – photographed in their pit yard, probably outside the fitting workshop or smithy. Large and heavy iron chains used for haulage or for taking great weights via pulleys can be seen suspended from a brick wall in the background; and a couple of small pulley wheels lean against the same building. Again, most of the miners are wearing 'nicky tams', string tied below their trouser knees. Maybe their soft caps were bought from the same source, as they look very similar! Waistcoats were commonly worn by pitmen at this time, and belt fasteners included the popular 'snake' clasp type just visible on the waist of the standing figure on the left. The youngest lad appears to have been given pride of place in the centre of the group. Before the introduction of state pensions it was not unusual for some miners to work well into their 70s, and occasionally 80s. However, on early photographs some miners look a lot older than their actual ages. The seated veteran shown on the right may only have been in his fifties or sixties. This image probably dates from about 1914 or a little later. *NUM*

This c.1890 image of a Durham miner shows the kind of old work clothes that were commonly worn in the industry over several generations. A clay pipe in his mouth, the man appears to be holding his waist band, which in turn is supporting a lamp, probably a type used by haulage lads in the North East known as a 'Midgy'. Made from tin, it had an open but hooded front, was carried upright and contained a lighted candle or an oil-soaked wick, the flame partly protected by a small lip extending a few centimetres upwards. The lamps had a short hook for attaching to clothes or elsewhere when working, especially in drift mines where the threat from gas was far less obvious. His trousers, crudely cut down to make long working shorts, are probably made from hessian or coarse wool, and almost reach stockings tied below the knee. Similar oil-wick lamps were used by Scottish miners, attached to their caps or belts.

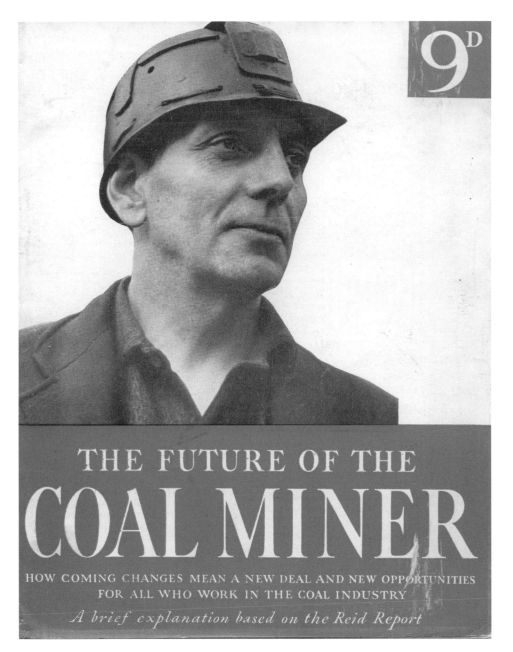

THE FUTURE OF THE COAL MINER

HOW COMING CHANGES MEAN A NEW DEAL AND NEW OPPORTUNITIES
FOR ALL WHO WORK IN THE COAL INDUSTRY

A brief explanation based on the Reid Report

9D

In September 1944, the Coalition Government set up an advisory committee under the chairmanship of Charles Reid 'to examine the present techniques of coal production from coal-face to wagon, and to advise what technical changes are necessary in order to bring the industry into a state of full efficiency'. The resultant Reid Report of 1945 was of great importance, contributing to a growing debate for state intervention and public ownership. The postwar reforming Labour government led by Clem Attlee went on to create the National Coal Board followed by the nationalisation of the industry on 1 January 1947. Commissioned by the Ministry of Fuel and Power, a 40-page illustrated booklet was published in a popular format, highlighting the main findings of the report. Its front cover shown here featured a 'modern miner' wearing a safety helmet.

MINING PEOPLE

NINEPENCE

Mining People was an interesting promotional booklet issued by the Miners Welfare Scheme (MWS) in 1945, in celebration of its 25th anniversary. Best known for the funding of pithead baths and canteens, the MWS also supported a wide range of health, sport and recreational facilities for miners and their families. The health element included help with and facilities for medical treatment and the funding of rehabilitation centres and convalescence homes. Education was also an important funding element of the Scheme, especially in relation to mining and technical schools and the provision of scholarships and grants to students. After 1952, a new body known as the Coal Industry Social Welfare Organisation (CISWO) took over, becoming a national charity in 1995. Today, around 350 miners' welfare schemes operate in former coalfield regions under CISWO.

COAL — THE N.C.B. MAGAZINE — MAY 1947 — 4^D

In May 1947 the NCB (in co-operation with the Ministry of Fuel and Power) launched its new magazine, *Coal*, produced by the Central Office of Information. The first cover photograph, shown here, featured 'a veteran of the pits' riding a paddy mail, with a couple of younger men just visible in the background. The experienced man was chosen 'as the living expression of the spirit of British mining [with] strength, patience and experience carved on his rugged face'. The miner was Fred Woolhouse, who worked at Silverwood colliery, near Rotherham in south Yorkshire. Fred had become something of a 'pin up', his image having been used earlier, in 1942, in the Forces magazine *Parade* where he was described as the 'Atlas on whose broad shoulders rests the whole of the fabric of Britain's industrial war effort'. A rope splicer and 'roadman' by trade, Fred, like many miners had horticultural interests, renting a piece of land from a farmer on which he grew vegetables and kept a few pigs and poultry, providing much needed food – in lieu of ration coupons – for his wife and 8 children during the war years.

Coal included a variety of human interest news items and stories that appealed to the general public as well as miners and their families. Functioning from 1947-1961, it was highly successful in this regard, and its early issues are now digitised and can be viewed via the National Coal Mining Museum for England's website (http:www.ncmonline.org.uk/). In 1961, *Coal* was transformed into *Coal News*, the 'newspaper of Britain's mining industry', publishing national as well as regional issues. It continued until the mid-1990s. The National Archives has a 92-volume set for the years 1947-1983 (ref: COAL71) as part of their NCB and British Coal archive. *Coal (vol 1, May 1947): National Coal Mining Museum for England (hereafter NCMME)*

In 1946, the new National Coal Board commissioned one of Britain's best portrait draughtsmen, H. Andrew Freeth RA, to produce a series of 'pit profiles' for their new magazine *Coal*. It proved to be an immensely important appointment, for Freeth went on not only to produce many superb images of miners but also provided very insightful pen portraits. Today, H.A. Freeth's legacy of portraits of miners is of considerable historical importance, well recognised by the National Coal Mining Museum for England. A recent exhibition there featured several of Freeth's profiles alongside 're-profiled' modern portraits of Kellingley miners by the photographer Anton Want. The examples that follow were published in some of the early issues of *Coal*.

The first Pit Profile by H.A. Freeth appeared in *Coal's* May 1947 issue and featured a 62-year-old Glamorgan miner Griffith Thomas, who had worked at Seven Sisters Colliery for forty years. Starting as a blacksmith, Thomas went on to assume 'full responsibility for the working of the complex machinery' at the pit. He was said to be proud that his six sons had followed him into mining, five as mechanical fitters at Seven Sisters. *H.A. Freeth & Freeth family archive*

H.A. Freeth was careful to include in his pit profiles examples from a variety of locations, including some from the smaller and less well-known coalfields. Sidney Hawkins, for example, was a Forest of Dean Free Miner. This meant that he was born in the Hundred of St Briavels and had worked for one year and day in a Forest of Dean mine. The ancient right allowed him to share royalties on all deep-mined coal in the Forest. Hawkins, born in 1886, started work at the age of 12 at the New Fancy Colliery, moving for a short time to Union Pit, before returning to his first colliery. Other collieries then had the benefit of his labour, including Eastern United and Lightmore, prior to settling at Princes Royal, where he was an overman, in 1922. Freeth carefully recorded some of Hawkins's comments as well as completing a compelling watercolour of the man. With his yardstick and carbide lamp in one hand, it is a very striking portrait (No.10 in the series). This is what Hawkins said about some aspects of his early mine work:

'We used to work more and we used to drink more then – we needed it. When you are working soaked through for six hours on end... drink's the only thing to keep you going. We had no pit-head baths – we used to walk home wet through with perspiration. Many's the time I've had to thaw my trousers out in front of the fire before taking them off.' *H.A. Freeth & Freeth family archive*

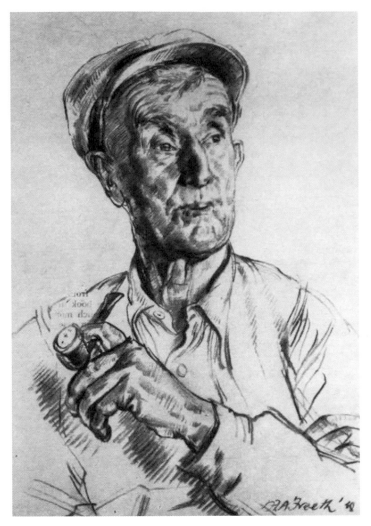

Here is what H.A. Freeth wrote about one of his Scottish sitters, that of the mining veteran, Charles Rowen (Profile No.16):

'His thin face, blue eyes, humorous mouth are as Scotch as they make them, while his accent – leaves the pure "foreigner", to say the least of it, dubious. Yet in spite of a difficulty which it must to be confessed is mutual, his story was pieced together.'

Freeth's written observations and astute commentary always complemented his artistic presentations. It is clear that like a great portrait photographer he had a natural way to communicate with and relate to working people.

Rowen had spent 55 years in the industry, starting at Langland Colliery, Maryhill, near Glasgow, working underground 'on the haulage', graduating to hand-got and then mechanical cutter coal on the faces. After a short spell in North Wales, he returned to Scotland, working at Bardykes pit and then Prestongrange Colliery, near Edinburgh, one of his posts there that of training officer. A Union delegate and Vice-President of Mid and East Lothain Miners' Association, Rowen was also active in public life, as an East Lothian County Councillor. *H.A. Freeth & Freeth family archive*

A Durham pitman, with an Irish surname, Faloon, was the subject of pit profile number 19 in 1948. Freeth shows Joseph Faloon in head and shoulders mode, facing the viewer, but to add interest he is glancing slightly to the right, with a faint image of part of his pit – Kibblesworth - in the background. Faloon had experience of most pit jobs before working at Kibblesworth, from pony-driving and 'putting' (pushing/pulling tubs) to filling (shovelling coal) and found himself back hand putting there, a very arduous task. He told Freeth that he lost two stones in weight in the first fortnight. Sticking it for almost 10 years, he then moved to Glamis pit, as a filler. Active in union affairs at Glamis, Faloon was said to be a great reader, his favourite authors being Keats, Shelley, Byron, Robert Service, Burns and Dickens; and his 'other passion' was listening to opera. Not bad going for an 'uneducated' lad who left school for the pit at fourteen. *H.A. Freeth & Freeth family archive*

Herbert 'Erby Enlegs' Humphrey worked at Tilmanstone Colliery, in Kent, when interviewed and painted by Freeth in 1949 (Profile 27); but as a young man he had worked in the metal mines of western USA, including a spell as a gold miner and water-pipe 'tunneller' for the city of Los Angeles. Pit-sinking in Scotland followed before moving to work in Kent, developing Betteshanger until 1929. After a short spell working near Doncaster, he returned to Kent, at his present pit, Tilmanstone. Freeth described Humphrey as 'a short man with a wrinkled forehead and a nose like the Duke of Wellington's when seen from the side'. In relaxed mode, sitting with his hands on his knees and dudley (water bottle) by his side, the informality of Freeth's portrait is a very clever arrangement, brilliantly complementing the worded character sketch. *H.A. Freeth & Freeth family archive*

A few months after painting Herbert Humphrey, Freeth featured a north Wales miner, George Evans, in his pit profile series (No.32). On this occasion it was the miner's face that was profiled, though, because of Evans's extraordinary family background in mining, he was also shown in entirety, alongside his remarkable great grandfather John Evans (see page 13). Freeth's opening remarks summed up Evans' in a few insightful words:

'You might say that George Evans physiognomy betrays his nature, while his voice reveals it. His rugged features, flattened nose, deep-sunk eyes, thin lips, almost cauliflower ears, all betoken the boxer. Yet his low voice is gentle and musical. As he speaks the impression of the pugilist fades and the more genuine impression of a quiet, retiring, reliable personality replaces it. Imagine his lilting Welsh voice talking to you.'
H.A. Freeth & Freeth family archive

COAL

THE N.C.B. MAGAZINE

MAR. 1948

4D

FIRST YEAR : SEE PAGE 6

British collieries attracted around 100,000 new recruits in the first year of nationalisation, a remarkable achievement. However, the NCB recognised that the number of boy entrants was relatively low in order to 'maintain the flow of new blood'. Consequently, the cover of the March 1948 issue of *Coal* was used to promote youth employment in the mines, and featured a young lad called Alan Wright, symbolically shown calling to his mates. Alan was a dataller (general, day-wage worker) from Dean and Chapter Colliery, Ferryhill, County Durham. What a thrill it must have been for him and his family after this image was published. *Coal (vol 1, March 1948): NCMME*

COAL
THE N. C. B. MAGAZINE
MAR. 1949

MINER'S GIRL
(see page 3)

6^D

The cover of the March 1949 issue of *Coal* featured the actress Dilys Jones, who played Glenis Thomas-Evans, a physiotherapist who falls in love with Tom Thomas (Emrys Jones), one of the main stars of the NCB-backed film *Blue Scar.*

Directed by the socialist documentary filmmaker Jill Craigie (wife of the Labour politician Michael Foot) and set in a south Wales mining village at the time of nationalisation, the film was well received by miners and the mining press. Its title was a reference to the blue wound marks seen on miners' skin as a result of embedded coal dust. *Blue Scar* was 'a realistic film of mining life' and 'refreshingly free from over dramatisation and false sentimentality', according to its review in *Coal*. Shot in a disused Port Talbot cinema and in the village of Abergwynfi, much of the sub-cast consisted of local people.

Many years later, in 2009, the film director's visit to Albion Colliery was recalled by 'Theo', via the forum of the excellent Welsh Coalmines website (www.welshcoalmines.co.uk). Theo, an apprentice mining surveyor, remembered the antics of his supervisor, Dai Davies who 'never wore a hard hat, always a cloth cap turned back to front when sighting through an instrument and more often than not would take it off and hang it on the side somewhere'. Miss Craigie, after encountering the surveyors at work, enquired as to why Dai was not wearing a safety helmet. Dai turned to Theo and said in very affected Oxford-style voice 'I say, would you be so kind as to pass me my hat, we have company.' The pit manager accompanying Craigie was not amused! *Coal (vol.2, March 1949): NCMME*

A future Scottish miner: wearing a helmet and cap lamp, this 16-year-old lad was a new recruit, attending a residential course at Middleton Camp, Gorebridge, Midlothian. The youth's mucky face and neck clearly show that he was already getting some practical instruction though there would be much more ahead – on the pit top and underground – at a nearby working pit. This image dates from 1950 when training was becoming much more organised under the recently formed National Coal Board (Scottish Division).

In order to conserve power supplies, largely due to the industrial action of coalminers, the Conservative government of Edward Heath had introduced a limit on energy consumption for commercial users, from 1 January 1974. The so-called three-day week was a time of candle shortages and cold dinners. Then, in the wake of Heath's 'who rules Britain' general election announcement, the miners went on strike on 7 February. The outcome was the defeat of the Conservatives and a hung parliament, Harold Wilson gaining a small majority in a second election held in October of the same year. The miners' strike had ended just two days after the February election following a settlement that included a substantial, 35%, pay award. This image is of an unnamed miner from Lady Windsor Colliery, situated at Ynysybwl, south Wales, photographed during the overtime ban that preceded the 1974 strike. Sinking at Lady Windsor started in 1884 and the high-grade coal produced was in great demand to fuel ships and steelworks, the pit employing around 1500 persons at its peak. From the 1970s, Lady Windsor and neighbouring Abercynon Colliery functioned as a single production unit but was closed by British Coal in 1988, three years after the 1984-85 strike, despite having considerable saleable reserves. No doubt the black-dusted face of the miner was soon cleaned in the pit's baths. Lady Windsor was one of the first mines in Britain to introduce bathing facilities, in 1931.

In 1969 the *Doncaster Gazette* carried out a 'fact-finding' survey of Doncaster's biggest pits. One of the collieries was Hatfield Main, then little more than fifty years old and managed by Ian Craig McGregor, pictured with a dust-grimed face and wearing his helmet and Oldham cap lamp. McGregor informed the reporter that his pit had received little capital investment, though skip installation was due to be introduced shortly, a facility that would reduce its manpower from around 1900 to 1750 'with a minimum of hardship'. He also spoke about the 'vast reserves' that 'we're very anxious to prove'. Not in his wildest dreams would have McGregor predicted that Hatfield – now (2015) owned by Hatfield Colliery Partnerships Ltd – would become Britain's last deep mine. *Doncaster Gazette/Aidan J. Bell*

From underground haulage lad to managing thousands of men, Aidan Jackson Bell has had an extraordinary career in mining, spanning the years from 1957 to 2003. A parson's son, but there is no doubt who stimulated his lifelong interest and career: an heroic grandfather from County Durham, William Bell. William was in the rescue team at the West Stanley (Burns pit) disaster in 1909 when 168 miners lost their lives. Thirty-three years later, aged 65, Bill had a narrow escape following an explosion at Barnsley Main when 13 men were killed. Unconscious and trapped from the blast, William Bell's trousers caught fire, causing his legs to twitch, a movement that alerted the rescue men to his demise.

Aidan started work at Haig pit in Cumberland at a time when 'pit lasses' were still employed on the surface. Hand-lashing and tramming tubs and work on the endless rope haulage system was followed by probably the best way to get to know a complex underground colliery: working with the surveyors as a linesman, measuring and marking in the roadways and workplaces, coal seams varying from a couple of feet to almost two yards, some extending five miles under the sea. Measuring up after accidents and fatalities would never be forgotten. Hand-got and machinery-based face training soon followed.

Under a well-known mentor, the Yorkshire mining engineer and manager John Ernest Longden, Aidan gained his management qualification at 25, probably the youngest in the country to do so at the time. Working as an under-manager and eventually deputy manager, during the 1960s he was able to obtain supervisory and practical experience from relatively short spells at several of Yorkshire's biggest mines: Rossington, Highgate (Goldthorpe), Bullcroft, Hickleton, Yorkshire Main and Goldthorpe-Highgate again. A bold step followed. Towards the end of 1969 Aidan emigrated to Zambia where he became production manager for four large copper mines employing 5,000 miners and 800 engineers. After seventeen years there he was back in Britain, in charge of a private pit near Stoke-on-Trent. The final management job was on the west coast of Scotland, at the Lochaline silica sand mine. Coalminers had many transferrable skills, well adapted to other mineral enterprises. Aidan certainly took advantage of his experiences and qualifications but will never forget his mining family history, one of his proudest possessions being lamps associated with his grandad, which he can be seen holding in his left hand; the other is Aidan's old 'Eccles' deputy's lamp, engraved with 'Mr Bell'.

Although Stephen Hamilton's career in mining was relatively brief, he has retained a direct and passionate interest in the industry right up to the present day, currently as a member of several community history groups. First and foremost a Cadeby Main man, Stephen also gained experience at nearby Manvers and Barnburgh pits. The son of a miner and one of seven mining brothers, Stephen's first job after leaving school aged 16 in 1969 was on the pit top, working in Cadeby's timber supply stockyard. Subsequent basic underground training included some of the traditional tasks of young miners: how to harness, equip and move a pit pony, opening and closing ventilation doors; and how to handle tubs. Once trained, his first proper job at Cadeby was working with the dust samplers, then progressing to coal face work via a variety of underground experiences. Talk to Stephen about his life in mining and he will certainly include his times as a flying picket, especially during the 1972 and 1974 strikes. It was the sudden death of a mate in an underground accident that was the main reason for leaving the industry at the end of 1979, though he continued to be active and supportive of the miners during the 1984/85 dispute; and indeed for many years afterwards. A talented artist and poet, Stephen is shown here alongside the Cadeby Memorial Group's display stand at Edlington (Yorkshire Main Trust's commemorative 30th anniversary miners' strike event) in 2014.

Chapter Two

Women and Children

Child miners are occasionally portrayed at commemorative events. This example of a 'girl miner' was photographed at a revived miners' gala held in Barnsley in 2004. Note the dudley (water container) and carbide cap lamp attached to her helmet. *Yorkshire Post*

The mortal remains of the Females are deposited in the Graves at the feet of the Males as undernamed.
1ᵗ Grave begining at the South end,
Catharine Garnett Aged 11 Years.
Hannah Webster Aged 13 Years.
Elizabeth Carr Aged 13 Years.
Ann Moss Aged 9 Years.
2ⁿᵈ Grave,
Elizabeth Hollings Aged 15 Years.
Ellen Parker Aged 15 Years.
Hannah Taylor Aged 17 Years.
3ʳᵈ Grave,
Mary Sellors Aged 10 Years.
Elizabeth Clarkson Aged 11 Years.
She lies at the feet of her Brother James Clarkson.
Sarah Newton Aged 8 Years.
Sarah Jukes Aged 10 Years.

Women and young children under the age of ten years were routinely used by many coal owners as part of their underground workforce until the landmark legislation – championed by Lord Ashley (7th Earl of Shaftsbury) – became law in 1842/43. Before then there are many cases of young persons killed in mines, perhaps the most notable concerning the Huskar pit at Silkstone near Barnsley when 26 girls and boys lost their lives, trapped whilst trying to escape from an inrush of water following a freak summer storm in 1838. Two faces of the commemorative obelisk sited at the edge of the village churchyard bear testimony to the tragedy, the youngest girls, Sarah Newton and Ann Moss, just 8 and 9 years old respectively. Ten-year-old George Birkinshaw died alongside his 7-year-old brother Joseph. The Wright brothers, Isaac (12) and Abraham (8) were interred next to Birkinshaws. Not surprisingly, commissioners came to Silkstone when gathering information for the Yorkshire part of the report that formed the basis of subsequent reform.

The three national and several regional coalmining museums have realistic displays relating to women and child miners, based on testimony from the 1842 report. Here are two creatively modelled life-size examples from the National Mining Museum Scotland – Andrew Young, an 11-year-old putter and Margaret Hipps, also a putter, aged 17. Andrew was employed at Arniston Colliery, in Stobhill, Cockpen parish, Midlothian. He had worked underground since the age of 9, hauling coal in 'slypes' or curved wooden boxes via a rope or chain harness, working from 4 am until 5 or 6 at night.

Margaret Hipps, from Stoney Rigg Colliery, parish of Polmont, Stirlingshire, also worked long hours, from 8 until 6, and occasionally to 10 at night; her employment interrupted for several months after the loss of a finger. Margaret described how she filled about 3 cwt of coal into a slype and then dragged the container away from the face by means of a chain attached to her waist.

This realistic representation of a boy putter or hurrier (various other terms were also used in the regions) can be seen at the Radstock Museum in Somerset. Here the lad drags away from the face a sledge containing coals. The absence of wheels and rails made this one of the most excruciating jobs imaginable but only one stop ahead of working as a hewer, the more experienced man who 'hand-got' the coal with picks and wedges from the seam. Thomas Batty, when aged 93 in 1840, recalled his work at Morpeth collieries, where he had started work at the age of six, later becoming a putter, earning nine pence a day for moving 72 corves (coal baskets) in a shift of 10-12 hours: 'There were no safety lamps and no rails... Boys seldom saw the light in winter,' he said.

Life as a boy (or girl) trapper – opening and closing ventilation doors – must have been the loneliest and at times most frightening job in a mine. It is not surprising that concentration waned and eyes closed when sat in almost complete darkness, with only the flame of a candle or burning oil wick for light, for around 10 hours a day. The large image is of 'Vance', a 15-year-old lad who had 'trapped' for several years in a West Virginia coal mine, earning 75 cents a day in 1908. The chalked graffiti on the door emerged when the photographic plate was developed.

The smaller image is of a British trapper from about the same period, opening the door to allow a tub of coal to be manually pushed along rails. I've interviewed several old miners who still remember doing this job when working in pits in the 1920s and 1930s.

This superb but carefully posed photograph dating from 1910 is of John Davies, aged 10, who worked as a door trapper in one of the pits in the Ferndale group, at Rhondda Cynon Taf in the Rhondda Valley of south Wales. He is shown above ground at the end of his first shift, black-faced, wearing a cap and old clothes; and displaying items of portable necessities, including a water bottle and oil lamp. What may be a badge on the left side lapel of his jacket may indicate he had joined the union. Later in the ownership of Powell Duffryn, Ferndale was a development by the D. (David) Davis company. The complex was closed by the National Coal Board in 1959. *South Wales Miners Museum*

Black faces were also 'badges of office', as can be seen in this photograph showing three Welsh boy miners from the Rhondda Fawr valley 'at home' after their first day underground. The lads hardly look big enough to wield the shovel, axe and pick that they hold. They are, left to right: William Thomas Williams, Harold Smallcombe and David Jones, and are about 12-13 years old. Taken in the backyard of 27 King Street, Gelli, in about 1910. *Stewart Williams Publishers*

In the early twentieth century the workforce of collieries could range from 10 to 70 plus years and this was occasionally illustrated when groups of miners were 'captured' and 'composed' on the pit top by intrepid local photographers. This detail is from a group of Rhondda (Pentre Colliery) workmen photographed in about 1890. Judging by their 'tools of the trade' they appear to be craftsmen but the three boys seated on the ground, especially the middle lad, were probably new starters. *Stewart Williams Publishers*

Detail from another early (c.1898) photograph showing a group of boy miners, on this occasion from Denby Colliery, near Ripley in Derbyshire. Most of the lads are posed with safety lamps. One youngster sitting on the front row, second left, could not keep still despite the photographer's instructions, hence his blurred features. Caps, old clothes, scarves and 'pit boots' were essential requirements. The minimum age to work underground was raised to twelve years in 1887 (and to thirteen in 1900), so some of these boys were barely 'legal'. After the landmark 1911 Coal Mines Act boys were not allowed underground younger than fourteen years, though exceptions and abuses continued for several years. Denby (Drury Low) Ltd, an early Victorian mine, was worked until 1968. *NUM (Derbyshire)*

New starters either too young to go underground or awaiting the opportunity to do so were employed on the 'screens' or 'picking tables', sorting and getting rid of 'slack' and dirt from the coal. It was a dirty, dusty, noisy and monotonous job. They often worked alongside old and disabled pitmen, even women; and all subject to the discipline of a 'corporal' or 'gaffer'. This c.1900 example is from St Hilda Colliery, South Shields (County Durham [now Tyne & Wear]), the regimented arrangement of the boys resembling that of a work group of young offenders or convicts. The gaffer with his stick was placed for action on the raised viewing platform. *F. Atkinson, The Great Northern Coalfield 1700-1900 (UTP, 1968)*

COAL

THE N.C.B.
MAGAZINE

FEB. 1950

6^D

"Screen" Beauties

Three 'screen beauties' were featured on the February 1950 cover of *Coal*. They were employed in Lancashire, at Lyme Pit, Haydock. The NCB's magazine's editor also mentioned the honour of a British Empire Medal awarded to screenworker Miss Charlotte Davies of Wigan, for 51 years' service. Then aged 64, Miss Davies must have started work as a thirteen-year-old in 1898-99. Although Wigan and Lancashire dominated, 'pit-brow' lasses, 'screen wenches' or 'tip girls' were also employed in fair numbers in Scotland, Cumbria, Staffordshire and south Wales. Britain's last pit-top women workers retired from Haig Colliery, Whitehaven as recently as 1972. *Coal (vol 3, February 1950): NCMME*

A group of 'breaker boys' from the Woodward coal mines in Kingston, Pennsylvania photographed in about 1900. New immigrant families often provided the very cheap labour. Working in open-sided sheds and without gloves, the boys had to break large chunks of coal into smaller uniform pieces and hand pick out any waste material. The minimum age of employment had been increased to 12 years in 1885 but the law was often not enforced. The practice continued until around 1920, photographic images a major factor in eradication of this form of child labour. Here they can be seen posing with their lunch boxes, a few of the younger boys looking down from coal wagons.

This somewhat romanticized image of Wigan 'work-girls' was published in one of the early editions of *Cassell's History of England*, published in the 1870s. Note the passing colliers, one of them glancing towards the women, and pit head gears, clearly drawn by someone with little appreciation of how they really worked.

In 1886, a mines bill formulated by Gladstones's Liberal Government and supported by the miners' male dominated unions included a clause that excluded women from pit-top work. This resulted in a furore of protest from the women and a fast-developing right to work campaign culminated in a well reported deputation of 23 women to the House of Commons and Home Office on 16-17 May 1887. The lobbying was a success. Apart from not being allowed to move heavy wagons, women were able to continue working as normal. *The Illustrated London News*'s engraving of the women, wearing their traditional work clothes, was based on an image produced by the well-known 'pit-brow' photographer Herbert Wragg of Wigan.

MILLARD Photo.   WIGAN.   MILLARD Photo.   WIGAN.

From the 1850s female 'pit lasses', particularly from the Wigan area of Lancashire, were carefully posed and photographed in studios (and later on site), the resultant small card-backed images known as cartes de visites sold to both locals and visitors. Larger cabinet versions, costing a little more, were also produced. The women and girls had become curiosities. The carte examples shown here are from a studio located opposite the New Market Hall, founded by James Millard. An unknown girl wearing her working clothes and clogs, her right arm resting on a shovel, is a typical example. Trousers worn under skirts, often patched and worn, testified to the cold and hard working conditions, and also added to their wider public interest: women wearing men's clothes, albeit for work, was very unusual. In the group image the women are each wearing very similar attire, even down to matching neck and head scarves; but, understandably, do not appear very relaxed.

In south Wales, Tredegar photographer A. Clayton took many interesting 'on site' images of mine or 'tip girls' as they were sometimes known. This extraordinary carte example of two young females shows them carrying what appear to be galvanised and spouted water cans and the tin water bottle and container balanced on their heads contributes to a very unusual composition. The uneasy stance of the girl on the right of the photograph is hardly helped by the long-handled pick that she rests on. *Gallery of Costume (Platt Hall): Manchester City Galleries*

As well as working on the screens women were also employed on a variety of pit-top haulage tasks, including the conveyance of wagons/tubs of coal – on rails – from the cages to their downward journey for sorting and cleaning, even operating the tipplers, the mechanism for tilting and emptying loads. Minor accidents at and around the pit-heads and in the yards due to trapped fingers and hands and falls were common; and fatalities were occasionally recorded. This extraordinary image from a print shows young women employed at a French mine, actually helping the unloading of wagons full of miners, their clothes 'standardised' by the artist.

From the early 1900s many thousands of postcard versions of studio photographs were published, again especially from the Wigan area. The original image for this example was published in a carte and cabinet format by Millard in the 1880s, and twenty or so years later issued as a popular postcard. This example from the author's collection was posted in 1904 as part of the Wrench Series and printed, as most early cards were, in Saxony (Germany). The carefully composed group, with one of the women holding a shovel and another a sieve, has great impact even today – despite the drab monochrome. Colour-enhanced versions of pit brow lasses were also issued in large editions by the card companies. Just look how Millard has placed the hands of the women, attention to detail was all important for commercial appeal. If not fashion icons, the women and girls captured the imagination of Edwardian society.

A miner's wife attends to her husband's bath before the kitchen fire, a common scene in coalfield communities from the 1850s through to the 1950s and beyond. Women and girls were the great unpaid workforce in mining, their never ending domestic choirs and responsibilities, from washing, cleaning and cooking to childcare meant very long and exhausting days. And then there was the constant fear of poverty, through strikes and disputes to sickness, incapacity and premature death. Living next to and amongst other families in similar situations provided some consolation, though goodness knows how so many coped, especially those with large families.

Britain's 1979 Coal Queen Debbie Johnson (21) models what was described as a 'space-age helmet destined for use by underground mineworkers'. Known as the Airstream, it protected the lungs and eyes as well as the head. Organised by the NCB and NUM, beauty contests were popular attractions at miners' galas and picnics, especially after nationalisation. Their 'escorts' – girls aged 2-7, could compete for the title of Miss Miner's Lamp. Regional winners went on to a national competition held in Skegness or Blackpool. The national Coal Queens received a holiday, watch and cash in recognition of their success. In return the girls and women were used in a variety of promotional events. A Coal Queen exhibition at the National Mining Museum for England in 2008 included reference to several former contestants.

Chapter Three

Pit Top

Getting rid of the muck and grime in the showers of the pithead baths. Much better here than at home!

OUT-CROPPING MIDHOPE.

Coal was unofficially mined via outcrops or 'day-holes' during strikes and disputes, the actual process not dissimilar to shallow workings in medieval times. Here the miners – with a great sense of humour – display some of their extracted coal in an old wooden box suspended from an impromptu branch or 'headgear', which they have named Shag's Main. Full sacks of coal suggest it was a successful enterprise. The hamlet of Midhope, in the parish of Bradfield, lies about 10 miles north of Sheffield, at the edge of the Peak District, and is now a conservation area. This image probably dates from 1912. *Chris Sharp/Old Barnsley*

Small private mines employing a few hands, known variously as drifts, adits and levels, continued to be a feature of the coal industry, even after nationalisation. No shaft descent was needed, just a walk into the workings. This superb postcard image shows a group of seven miners outside the entrance to their hillside drift mine, displaying a tub load of impressively large lumps of coal. Most of the men have carbide lamps attached to their caps; one young lad displays a long hand drill and another more mature man holds a pick. The high quality coal was extracted by hand-got work in the old style. Probably photographed in Lancashire, c.1905.

Headstocks, also known as headframes were usually constructed of timber until the 1912 Coal Mines Act when any *new* installations had to be steel-based structures. This example, from a Barnsley area colliery, is of fine quality. The massive and sturdy timbers, probably of pitch pine, even have architectural features such as corbels usually associated with stone buildings. A plain-looking stone or brick winding engine house can be seen in the background and the whole site dominated by a tall brick-built chimney, just in view. Part of the cage used for taking men and materials up and down the shaft is just visible within the base of the headstocks, as are some of its supporting chains. The timber-framed structure on the right, part of the heapstead, provided some shelter for workers to sort and grade the coal. What really makes this excellent image, however, are the pit-top haulage team pictured with two of their horses, one actually harnessed and linked to a couple of wagons. The man on the extreme left appears to be of some authority, as does the person displaying the unattached horse, perhaps the senior stableman or ostler. Interestingly, what appear to be gas lanterns are sited on either side of the headframe, providing some form of illumination on dark days and at night. A chalked noticeboard is attached to the lower face of one of the upright timbers, just above head height, maybe an instruction re cage-riding capacity. Thus there is much of interest on this splendid early photograph dating from about 1890.

Flour Mills Colliery. Forest of Dean, Glos. S.D. Real Photo Series. 540

Groups of miners can be seen around the pithead of Flour Mill Colliery in the Forest of Dean in this image, created for a Gloucestershire postcard. The men in the foreground have clearly responded to the photographer and are enjoying a smoke before the start of their shift. The cages here were quite small, so numerous draws via the steam winding engine would be required. The yard, set in pleasant countryside, is typical of many smaller collieries, strewn with timber, tubs and what appear to be iron pumps, a scene realistically recreated in the north of England at the Beamish Living Museum in County Durham. Although only a small coalfield, by 1912 the Dean had 8,525 miners via its ancient and unique tradition of free miner ownership and regulation. Flour Mill was one of the larger deep mines or gales as they were known, employing as many as 700 men and boys at the strike of 1909 after which it closed for a time. Beset with water problems and linked underground to neighbouring Princes Royal colliery, the last coal extracted directly from Flour Mill was not long after the General Strike and lockout of 1926.

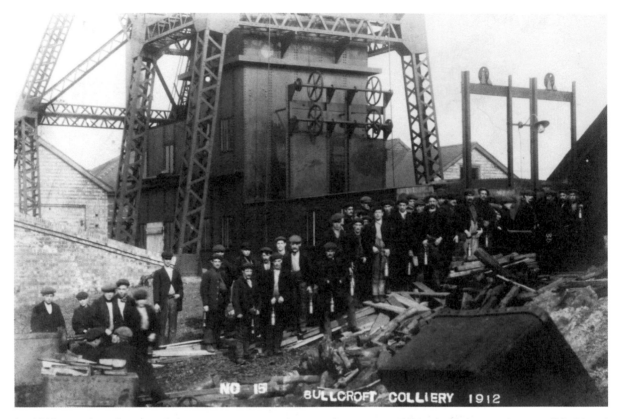

In 1912 a series of postcards by an anonymous photographer were published relating to the new 'Markham' colliery located near Carcoft village in the rapidly expanding Doncaster coalfield. For view number 15, miners turn to face the photographer at what soon became known as Bullcroft Main Colliery, owned and developed by the well-known colliery and engineering entrepreneurs, the Markham family, from north Derbyshire. Standing on a temporary bank of planks and carrying their lamps, the men and boys are about to start their shift underground, dwarfed by the base of the great steel lattice frame of Bullcroft's new headstocks, which had replaced a sturdy but temporary timber structure set up for a difficult period of sinking a few years earlier. A good number of the experienced men seen here would have been recruited from Markhams' Derbyshire businesses. The famous Barnsley seam was reached at the end of 1911 at a considerable depth of 662 yards so this group of miners would have been part of the first production shifts. A year later, a thousand men and boys were employed, a figure that rose quickly to 2,500 when output reached 24,000 tons a week. Direct production from 'Bully' ceased in 1970, its coal now extracted via a new underground link to neighbouring Brodsworth Colliery.

Once established, the more successful collieries also developed thriving ancillary industries such as brickworks and byproduct plants. Owners bought or leased more land and what were once modest sites in rural settings became unmistakable complexes. The addition of tall chimneys in valley locations became an integral part of a new industrial scene at the edge of villages. Silverwood Colliery, near the village of Thrybergh, Rotherham, was developed from 1900 by Dalton Main Collieries Limited and by 1909 employed a huge workforce of 3,228, based entirely on the Barnsley seam of coal. This rare postcard image was published by the enterprising photographic family of Gothard of Barnsley, noted for their 'disaster' compilations. Steeplejacks sit nonchalantly on a secured platform near the top of the 180 foot-high chimney which had been 'pointed hooped and fitted with a lightning conductor by A.M. Wilkinson Sheffield', according to the information written on the reverse of the card. Four other intrepid workmen can be seen, despite the presence of what appear to be attached ladders, dangling from ropes about halfway up the structure. Fred Dibnah would have enjoyed seeing this Edwardian view. Silverwood survived the miner's strike by ten years, finally closing at the end of 1994 and much of its old coal tip is now a nature reserve. A memorial to the miners who worked there was unveiled on the site in 2013.

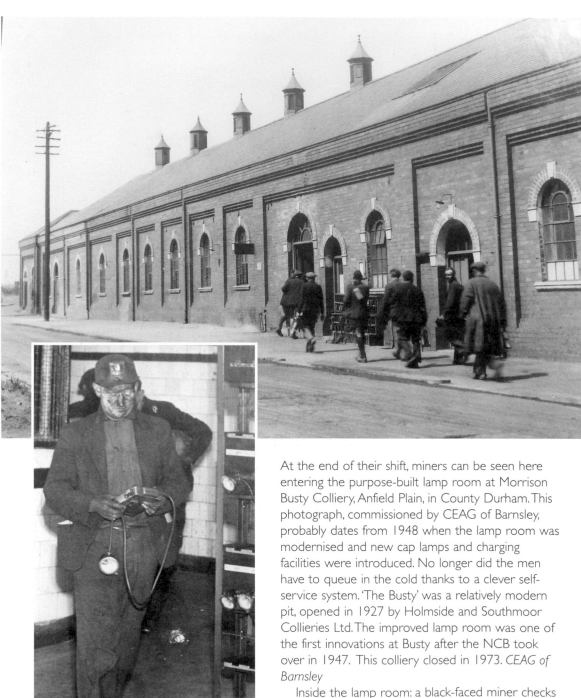

At the end of their shift, miners can be seen here entering the purpose-built lamp room at Morrison Busty Colliery, Anfield Plain, in County Durham. This photograph, commissioned by CEAG of Barnsley, probably dates from 1948 when the lamp room was modernised and new cap lamps and charging facilities were introduced. No longer did the men have to queue in the cold thanks to a clever self-service system. 'The Busty' was a relatively modern pit, opened in 1927 by Holmside and Southmoor Collieries Ltd. The improved lamp room was one of the first innovations at Busty after the NCB took over in 1947. This colliery closed in 1973. *CEAG of Barnsley*

Inside the lamp room: a black-faced miner checks the number on his cap lamp battery, so that he can replace it in the correct position on the charging stand, another CEAG image from the late 1940s. *CEAG of Barnsley*

The great winding engine at Lady Victoria Colliery, Newtongrange, Midlothian. Steam-powered, it was made and installed by Grant, Ritchie and Company of Kilmarnock in 1894. The engineman sat and operated the mechanism from the chair seen on the right. The huge winding drum around which the steel winding rope was attached to the cages has a formidable presence. Skilled winding enginemen were vitally important employees at collieries; it was an extremely responsible job where concentration was vital and the role often spanned several generations of the same family. Winding enginemen also had their own trade union or association. Winding engine house interiors were invariably kept spic and span and well maintained in periods of 'inactivity'. This massive engine is now a key exhibit at the preserved Victorian colliery, part of the Scottish Mining Museum.

A winding engineman (Tom Ashton) and his young assistant (Willie Thorp) at work at No.2 pit of the New Monckton colliery complex, at Royston, near Barnsley, in c.1930. Here, there appears to be a 'double chair' for the operators. Notice the kettle in the foreground! Enginemen could inflict a 'bad ride' on miners who had caused some offence, according to oral testimony.

Photographed in 2010, Richard Philips inside the driver's cabin in the winding engine house at Big Pit, the National Coal Museum for Wales, part of the Blaenafon World Heritage Site. This mine got its name from its exceptionally large elliptical shaft which allowed two drams of coal to be loaded into the cage side-by-side. The now electric winder has modern safety systems and computerised controls but winding enginemen such as Richard remain key figures in its operation. Since 1983 visitors have been able to descend the 90 metres (300 feet) of Big Pit's shaft for an underground tour, wearing standard miners' equipment and accompanied by a guide.

Blacksmiths were probably the most versatile of pit-top (and as and when required pit-bottom) workers, making, maintaining and repairing a variety of iron and metalware items, including horseshoes. They functioned from workshops that contained from one or two forges to batteries or rows of forges at the larger collieries. Here, in 1908, the 'smiths and their strikers have assembled for a 'team' photograph at the Glamorgan Colliery, Llwynypia, in the Rhondda, several of them proudly displaying the tools of their trade. This large colliery was owned and developed by the respected Scottish engineer and entrepreneur Archibald Hood but had just become part of the Cambrian Combine Company. It was the scene of violent confrontations during the Tonypandy Riots of 1910-11, which included the deployment of the Metropolitan Police and troops, authorised by the Home Secretary, Winston Churchill. After the disturbances of November 1910 a squadron of the 18th Hussars were actually stationed at Glamorgan Colliery. Two striking miners swam through flooded workings in order to feed the pit ponies during the dispute. A year or so before the outbreak of the First World War some 3,907 men and boys were employed, making it a very substantial complex. The colliery did not, however, survive as a production unit after the Second World War and nationalisation, closing in August 1945. *Stewart Williams Publishing*

It wasn't unusual for there to be media interest when miners returned to work after a strike and any photographs taken not only drew attention locally to particular collieries and conditions of work but was also useful 'copy' for international distribution. This image, for example, was taken for an American readership, under a banner or caption of MINERS GO BACK TO WORK and dates from 29 February 1972. Miners had been out for seven weeks. Crammed into the cage, ready to descend for the morning shift, are a group of young Welsh miners at Penrikyber Colliery, near Aberdare, Glamorgan. Formerly part of the great Powell Duffryn company, the colliery had undergone major modernisation in 1963 and had a workforce of over 800 by the early 1970s. Penrikyber closed on 8 October 1985, shortly after the end of the great strike of 1984/85, ending over 110 years of production.

A small group of Lancashire miners duck their heads and blink in the bright light of day after disembarking from their cage at the end of a shift at Chanters No 1 pit, Atherton, in 1905. The lad at the front only looks 12 or 13 years old but manages to carry his lamp and water can without too much trouble. Caps were common then, as were old clothes and clogs or 'pit boots' but the youngster is well-wrapped up, so maybe worked in the cold pit bottom, linking and/or loading tubs of coal into the cage. Opened in the 1850s, Chanter's closed in 1966, during Lord Robens' chairmanship of the NCB. *NUM*

Before entering the locker room, two Welsh miners have their boots 'whirled' to remove as much dirt as possible. The notice reads 'BOOTS SHOULD NOT BE BRUSHED AFTER GREASING'. This image dates from 1959 and was one of a short series under the theme of 'Man in the Mine' used for publicity purposes and international distribution. Notice the old clothes worn, well before the NCB introduced free sets of standard orange-coloured workwear from the late 1970s. Hard hats were used in some pits from the 1930s, introduced from the USA into Scotland by Sir William Reid but in most instances had to be paid for entirely or in part by the wearers. Safety helmets became compulsory and freely issued after nationalisation, though they were not always popular in certain working conditions.

Following the Health and Safety Act of 1974 the NCB embarked upon a major series of safety campaigns, backed up with posters, literature, targets and publicity photographs above and below ground. This pit-top example is believed to have been taken at Whitwell Colliery in north Derbyshire and probably shows the manager and two miners whose attention is drawn to the H&S poster featuring a Kitchener-style 'Your Country Needs You' image. Notice the modern concrete-enclosed headgear in the background of the photograph, probably part of the No 2 shaft casing. Production ceased here in 1986 and signs of the colliery quickly eradicated from the local landscape after almost a century of existence.

Coalminers were often portrayed as 'curiosities' in the popular press during Victorian times. A young woman is seen sponging her father's back, the kneeling man leant over a tub of water in this engraving, from *The Graphic*, published on 18 February 1871. A smartly-dressed male is seen casually standing by the doorway and reading a newspaper. The reporter had this to say about the miners 'cleaning up after work':

'It is a common thing on a Saturday afternoon to see a collier in his 'back yard "getting weshed." The miner tubs about once at least once a week...The collier comes home as black as a chimney-sweep, and it is impossible that he can soap his own back.

He has been lying on his side probably half-naked in a close heading for many hours for the wages which he has brought home for his "missus," and, if she is a good wife with true womanly instincts, she quite understands the importance morally and physically of that tubbing.'

In the smaller image, recreated at the Scottish Mining Museum, a miner is seen washing from a zinc bath in front of the fire. Well into the twentieth century some miners were reluctant to have their backs washed too often, fearing it would take away some of their strength, even avoiding the showers in the pithead baths.

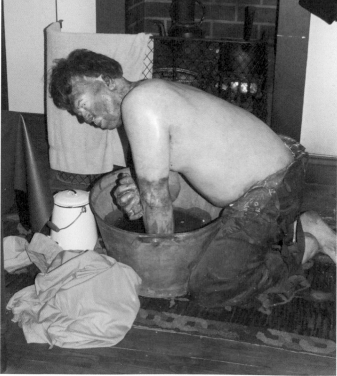

The introduction of purpose-built pithead baths, thanks largely to the Mines Act of 1920 and the establishment of the Miners' Welfare Fund, was one of the most important health and social innovations for thousands of miners; and was a massive help to women in the home. Females, the great unpaid workforce in mining, no longer had to spend hours boiling water and suffering from back and muscle ailments – even miscarriages – though domestic life remained far from easy. Locker rooms for dirty and clean clothes were provided, the miners paying a small weekly sum towards their upkeep. At some pits, instead of lockers there was a system of work clothes suspended via numbered chains, as can be seen in this example.

Miners appear happy enough when showering after work at a Stoke-on-Trent colliery on 9 January 1974. But all was not well in the coalfields of Britain and a three-day week had been recently imposed by the Conservative Government. This press image originated because of a meeting between the Employment Secretary, Willie Whitelaw and the NUM executive in the hope of solving an ongoing wages dispute. Included in a list of concerns by the miners was 'bath-time'. The night before, Prime Minister Edward Heath had created a new Department of Energy, headed by Lord Carrington. The talks and 'improvements' did not stop a coal strike and the ultimate demise of the Conservative government in a 'who governs Britain' snap general election. Coal production resumed on 11 March after a 16-week work to rule and 4-week strike by the miners, Harold Wilson's Labour Government now in power, albeit on a minority basis.

Another much appreciated innovation for miners was the provision of a proper pit-top canteen. Redbrook Colliery (a revamped Barnsley area pit) canteen was officially opened in 1970, when a group of miners toasted the NCB press photographer who duly recorded the occasion. It looks as though Albert Hirst's famous pork pies were on sale. From a mug of tea and a bottle of milk to a decent meal, for the first time miners could enjoy facilities that had been available in factories and offices for many years.

The position of 'weighman' was a crucially important pit-top job before nationalisation as their role was linked to miners' wages and the company's profits. In this image the formidable Denby (Drury Lowe, Derbyshire) weighman is seen on the extreme right and next to him is the checkweighman appointed and paid by the miners' association. In theory this was a necessary balance when coal weight and rates of pay were calculated and agreed. The weighbridge notices relate to shaft signalling and 'no smoking'. A tub containing high quality and large pieces of company coal is paraded in front of the weighbridge. *NUM*

A group of colliery craftsmen assemble for a c.1908 postcard image in front of the weighbridge at Sharlston Colliery, near Wakefield, west Yorkshire. Perhaps one or more of these worked in and around the weighbridge. Sharlston deep mine closed in 1993 but the land was outcropped by UK Coal during 2007-10, including landscape restoration of the site. *Norman Ellis*

The best thing about mining was getting paid, according to many of the miners that I have interviewed. For some it was Friday afternoon, whilst others got their cash on Saturday mornings. Under the old butty system a collier paid out his team of men at various locations, from pit yards to – very temptingly – pub yards; but many had to queue at the pay office, sometimes their money placed in a numbered 'tipple tin'. Contrasting images here for one of Doncaster's premier big pits, Brodsworth. The early photograph shows a line of men and boys waiting to be paid after the last shift of the week at a temporary pay office made of corrugated iron, not long after production had begun in about 1908. In stark contrast, smartly-dressed and expectant miners wait on the pit top on payday a few years later.

Chapter Four

Underground

A young lad takes care of his pony in its underground stable. 'Pony-driving' was one of the first and most responsible jobs that young miners experienced.

This early (c.1900) pit bottom scene features a 2-deck iron or steel cage (lift), clearly demonstrated here for the transport of men. Narrow shafts meant that double or even treble decks were advantageous, reducing the time of travel and number of 'draws'; but for the riders it was a cramped and uncomfortable journey, some of them unable to stand to their full height. The banksman at the pit top would 'load' the men on board at the start of their downward journey and liaise with the winding engineman as part of the process. Notice, the apparent total absence of any safety bar(s) other than the handrail in the lower deck. These men have the look of officials and/or managers rather than everyday miners and would have been well aware of the photographer. This is one of a remarkable series of lantern slides found in the early 1980s and converted to postcards by the Yorkshire Area NUM; however, the location was probably in a South Staffordshire colliery. The man just visible in the background, standing by a tub, may have been waiting to place or 'run-on' tubs of coal on to the cages; but if he was the on-setter (or 'pit-botommer') he would have been in charge of the loading of men and materials in and out of the cages, communicating with the surface banksman, and the winding engineman, by a series of hand-operated signals. Coal and miners were not *supposed* to travel in the same cage. Wire ropes attached to a 'twin' cage can be seen on the right. The two cages would pass each other at mid-journey. The scene looks primitive but it was far better than the old system of miners having to get up and down shafts by clinging to a rope or corve (basket), literally dangling into blackness. And here we can also see an early example of what appears to be electric lighting suspended from the roof space. *NUM(Yorks)*

Another early image from the South Staffordshire coalfield showing a team of colliers undercutting (or 'holing out') with picks in the Thick Coal seam, their confined working spaces protected by short timber props or 'sprags'; and the man standing on the right may be hand-drilling, in preparation for a shot. The face would be brought down in its entirety by a blast, so the coal might be in small and random sizes; however, smaller firing shots meant bigger pieces of coal and 'getting' by hand, though very arduous, offered even more control of coal-size. The final task was hand loading the coal into tubs or wagons. Interestingly, candles can just be discerned, probably secured in small balls of clay in the work areas. These coalface conditions and practices were little different to those evident throughout much of the nineteenth century. *NUM(Yorks)*

A close-up view of three miners working a low seam using traditional hand methods of mining, reproduced as a c.1908 postcard by a Welsh publisher, S. Timothy, but the image may date from about 1890. Two hewers can be seen using sharp-pointed picks (known as mandrels or mandrils in Wales) to get to the coal or undercut the coal, one of them on his side in an almost foetal position. The men are using peg and ball oil-wick lamps attached to their caps – in general use in levels or drift mines in South Wales at this time – and well visible on the cap of the man on the extreme right who is using a long-handled hammer to drive a wedge into the coal. A wedge and another hammer is just visible in the foreground. The lamps were far from ideal in low seams as they protruded and might catch the roof or any overhang. Notice the primitive but effective timber roof support, clearly part of the trunk or branch of a small tree. The fallen coal would here be scooped up in a 'curling box' and loaded into a wheeled 'dram' or small wagon for transporting to the pit bottom. This image is believed to be in the level or drift at Pentre Colliery in Ton Pentre, Rondda Fawr. *S. Timothy*

These two photographs really do show how difficult it could be to hand-fill coal into the tubs or drams when working in cramped conditions.

The lower image is from Ashington Colliery (Northumberland) in 1936, candles still in use, as can be clearly seen. In the background, part of a pony and its driver/haulier is just visible. The tub appears to be well-filled with coal, making it a very heavy load to manoeuvre and then transport.

In the upper image the miner appears to be hand-loading massive pieces of coal on to a wheeled open-backed wooden tub. Use of the rake ensured that small pieces of coal – of little value to the companies – were not loaded, falling through the twines, and discarded into the waste area known as the 'gob'. Filling using rakes was regulated in Derbyshire mines, this example in Denby pit. 'Against the rules' shovelling might result in instant dismissal. Whatever the situation, hand-filling coal was a 'back-breaking' job.

Pushing or pulling tubs of coal away from the coalfaces was one of the hardest jobs in mining before mechanization, usually taken on by young lads who aspired to be colliers and therefore earn more money. The regional terms that they were known as included 'drawers', 'putters', 'trammers' and 'hauliers'. Here are three early photographic examples, from c.1890-c1900. Candles were often attached to the tub end, embedded in a clay blob, providing a little light for a far from smooth journey.

On low roadways a lad, especially if he was new to the job, would catch his back on the roof, his wounds and bruises showing up at 'back-wash' time, much to the concern of mothers and sisters.

The use of ponies and horses enabled faster movement of tubs of coal from the direction of 'inbye' (the coalface) to 'outbye' (to the pit bottom); and of course greater loads could be moved. The young 'drivers', often with minimal training, were expected to treat the animals that they had taken charge of with care. There were only 8 horse inspectors in

1913, responsible for the welfare of 70,000 pit ponies, so ill-treatment, injuries and deaths occurred; but generally speaking there was a good relationship between drivers and ponies. Although the riding of ponies was not allowed, some lads tried their luck 'cowboy' and 'indian'-style, leaning as flat as possible on top of their backs. Deputies had ways and means of catching them out, including hiding in man-holes at the side of roadways and splashing the galloping youths with whitewash, a certain proof for an official in the pit bottom to administer a warning, clipped ear or fine. Here (upper image) a young driver sits on the 'limmers' and takes a train of 'full uns' to the pit bottom. From one of several postcards relating to Brayton Colliery (No.4 pit) published by John Patterson of Aspatria, c.1910.

Young 'putters' with their 'steeds' photographed for a postcard (lower image), also probably by Paterson of Aspatria, in about 1910. These lads worked at No 4 (Wellington) pit, one of five under the title of Brayton Domain Colliery, located at Aspatria in Cumberland, owned by Joseph Harris. In 1914 No 4 had 374 miners working underground and in 1915 seven men were killed in an underground explosion at Brayton. From 1912 until at least the 1930s this colliery was managed by Thomas Eadie who may have known the pony drivers pictured here. The Yard Band of coal, about 4-5 feet thick, was worked at Brayton until exhaustion in 1933.

Although deep in a West Virginia (USA) mine, this remarkable underground picture from 1908 showing two teenage pony lads holding on to their horse is fairly typical of British mines of the period. But notice the 'torches' (for light) that they typically wore on their caps despite the associated dangers.

The 1911 Coal Mines Act is regarded as a 'pit ponies' charter' but it was not really until after the nationalisation of the mines and legislation published in 1949 that the welfare of these animals was addressed and acted on in great detail. This image of a miner and pony was used to illustrate the front cover of *Pit Pony*, an official booklet issued by the National Coal Board in 1952. 'Bob' is proudly displayed alongside his handler Jim Childs outside Cannock Wood Colliery, part of the West Midlands Division of the NCB. The ponies were often exhibited, Bob twice winning Horse of the Year at Royal Shows. By 1951 the numbers of ponies used in collieries had declined to 15,500 and by the 1980s the few that remained in service were in small licensed mines.

Here are scenes that many miners will recognise, taking a 20-minute break and having some 'snap'. The upper image shows two French miners sitting on logs in a timbered roadway in the 1970s. No sign of any lunch container here, so maybe the bread was wrapped in paper and kept in the canvas bag just visible. 'Unprotected' snap attracted a variety of vermin and was the target of intelligent pit ponies!

The lower image is even more recognisable, the men eating from what appears to be an 'Acme' lunch tin, ingeniously rounded at one end to help it being popped into a jacket pocket. A variety of other regional names were used for miners' snap containers including 'bait tins' and 'tommy boxes'. In British mines jam and beef dripping were popular sandwich fillings, though one Cornish-born coalminer told me that his home-made pasties took some beating, so much so that he did a roaring trade with them in Bentley Colliery, near Doncaster.

This astonishing photograph dating from about 1920 shows two young haulage lads (and another in the team just visible in the background) pausing for the camera, working almost naked. The chain attached to the full tubs would have been hauled mechanically along the ringed roadway towards the pit bottom. Conditions appear wet underfoot. This image really does demonstrate the dirty and dangerous nature of pit work even in relatively modern times. Trapped or even severed fingers might occur when linking the trains of tubs. Believed to be at Chislet Colliery, originally an Anglo-German enterprise, taken over by British owners after the Great War. One of the four biggest pits in the Kent coalfield, Chislet was located near Canterbury, working until 1969. These men are not named but may have been Welsh as this relatively new coalfield attracted miners from south Wales and there was Welsh interest in the ownership and development of the mine.

The introduction of 'endless haulage' systems in coal mines resulted in faster and greater volumes of coal being extracted. A long steel rope passing around a pulley was rotated by an engine operated by a driver. Tubs could be attached singly or in sets. Two rail tracks were used, one for the 'empties' travelling inbye and one for the 'full 'uns' hauled outbye, so a wide and relatively flat roadway was required. As can be seen in this excellent piece of artwork by ex-Barnburgh (Doncaster) miner Bill Bennett, the linking process still involved a good deal of manual dexterity. *Bill Bennett*

The 'Paddy Mail' was another essential system of underground haulage, principally for man-riding so as to allow the miners to get inbye to workplaces without a long walk; and of course return outbye to the pit bottom at the end of the shift. The upper, older image, shows miners riding a basic tram haulage system, hauled by steam-powered rope to the pit bottom at the end of their shift at the Clay Cross Company pit in north Debyshire. The lad at the front, wearing rubber gloves – and a tie! – is the electrician, Albert Wragg. The modern c.1980 image shows miners riding the paddy in a Yorkshire pit. Although paddy accidents were rare, even with modern locomotive-powered systems multiple injuries and fatalities might occur, as happened at two Yorkshire pits: Silverwood Colliery in 1966 and Bentley in 1978.
NUM(Derbyshire)

Not only did Irvin Harris (1912-96), the son of a Yorkshire pit-sinker, have a remarkable career in mining including 20 years as a pit deputy, but from the 1940s he combined his work with a great passion for photography, producing some superb underground images to professional standards. This is a self-portrait, showing Irvin filling coal by hand. The scene is atmospherically and cleverly lit by his electric cap lamp and oil-flamed safety lamp which stood nearby; and would have involved a long exposure of 5-10 seconds – no flash of course. This was one of his 'unofficial' photographs, Irvin eventually getting permission from the coal company and the NCB to take photographs but subject to certain safety conditions. *Irvin Harris Collection*

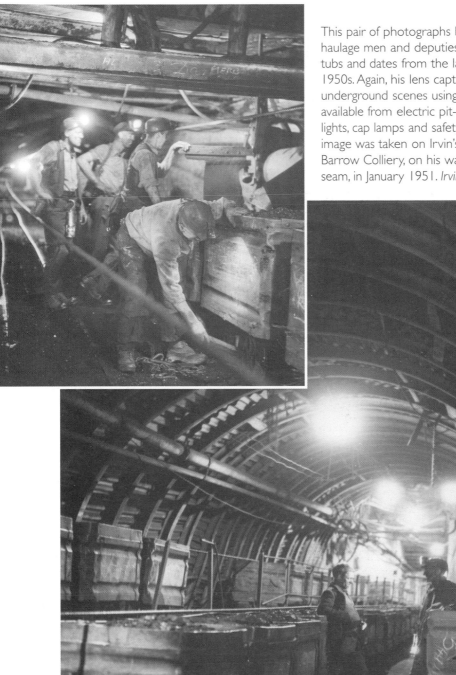

This pair of photographs by Harris shows haulage men and deputies attending to coal tubs and dates from the late 1940s and early 1950s. Again, his lens captures the underground scenes using what light was available from electric pit-bottom roof/wall lights, cap lamps and safety lamps. The lower image was taken on Irvin's last day of work at Barrow Colliery, on his way to the Fenton seam, in January 1951. *Irvin Harris Collection*

This extraordinary photograph dating from the 1930s or 1940s shows a miner wearing 'water gear' and knee pads crawling under a very wet face at Canderigg Colliery, Larkhill, Lanarkshire. The seam appears to barely more than a foot or so in height. Although in relatively modern times, he is still using a carbide lamp attached to his cap and has remarkable confidence in the short timber roof supports. This James Nimmo & Co pit closed in 1954, employing an average workforce of 379.

The rate of mechanisation of coalfaces was very patchy, varying from coalfield to coalfield, from pit to pit in the same region or NCB Division; and even in a single colliery it was not unusual for old hand-got methods to continue 'alongside' machinery-based, even power-loading systems. The illustrations on the next page are interesting early examples of coal-cutting machines. *Scottish Mining Museum*

Shirts-off, two miners operate a Samson coal-cutting machine after 'a weight' had closed down the face in the North Thorncliffe Seam at Barrow Colliery, near Barnsley in 1948. By the 1960s, Barrow was a leading exponent of mechanised faces and began to break Yorkshire, British and European output records.

The Thorncliffe Seam in particular was targeted to achieve 1,000 tons a day on a regular basis via a three-shift system of operation. Coal-cutting machines had been pioneered in several Yorkshire collieries from as early as the 1860s, with Wharncliffe Silkstone described as 'the largest user... in England' in 1892 advances and in Scotland followed, some 22 per cent of coal extracted in the Scottish coalfields by machine. Overall, however, the average output of machine-cut coal in Britain was only 8.6 per cent in 1913. *Irvin Harris Collection*

Wearing shorts and shirtless, an experienced miner operates a longwall coal cutter, probably in the Barnsley Seam, at Rossington Main. Mechanisation at the Doncaster-area pit had begun during the 1930s when Rossington was a part of Yorkshire Amalgamated Collieries group, and accelerated during the 1950s after nationalisation. The last hand-filled face closed here in 1964, all faces from then on power-loaded. Exceptionally, Rossington, albeit in a contracted form, continued to produce coal until its final closure in 2007.

Well into the 1980s miners continued to use age-old methodology with modern equipment. Here, lying on his side, Jimmy Dane drills into a thin seam of coal prior to the use of explosives in Emley Colliery in West Yorkshire.
Jeff Poar

In 1953 a revolutionary coal-cutting machine invented by James Anderton, the NCB production manager for the St Helens Area (Lancashire) was patented and became widely known as the Anderton Shearer Loader. As the machine progressed along longwall faces it sliced – or 'sheared' – a section of coal and via its forward and return run coal was deflected onto a conveyor. By the late 1970s about 80 per cent of coalfaces were worked by cutter-loaders. This c.1979 example is from Bentinck Colliery in south Nottinghamshire. Notice the hydraulic props, providing a canopy above the heads of the miners and huge teeth of the cutting drum – far removed from the picks of the 'hand-holers' of early miners.

Examples of shearer-loaders can be seen at national and regional mining museums, this realistic display (lower image) is from the National Mining Museum Scotland.

One obvious drawback for the miners was that the 'Iron Man' machines reduced the number of face workers needed. There were also health and safety issues, not 'just' in terms of personal injury but, long-term, because of the noise and dust generated by the operations. Disputes also emerged concerning pay-rates and payments for removing muck and debris from the new cutters. This illustration shows a Cadeby Main miner, Stephen Pratt, 'clearing the workplace' (from 21s coalface, Haigh Moor Seam) on 4 February 1975, an image that was in fact carefully created in support of an NCB safety campaign. *Stephen Pratt/Hamilton*

Although many pits were closed during the 1970s and especially after 1985, great efforts were made to create new drifts and headings in order to extend the life and make more productive what remained of the coal industry. Here, at Bullcliffe Wood, near West Bretton in West Yorkshire just two men can be seen using powered drills to move the tunnel forward, a large mechanical digger moving the resultant debris. Notice the steel rings, vitally important for safe progression; and also the numerous drill marks on the rock face. This was about 20 metres down the Calder Drift, according to a miner who worked there. Bullcliffe closed in 1985.

This spectacular image shows a huge drivage or road-heading machine paused whilst creating a new and wide underground roadway at Thorne Colliery, the most easterly mine of the Yorkshire coalfield. Although Thorne had recently merged with Hatfield Main it was 'mothballed' in 1988 and any hope of development was finally abandoned in 2002, despite around £34 million spent on surface and underground improvements in the 1980s; and the known presence of many thousands of tons of reserves in the High Hazel and Barnsley seams. The boom-type of machine has a massive rotating head containing numerous picks, the actual teeth of the great rock-cutting process.

Driveage workers and 'rippers' at Kiveton Park Colliery, near Rotherham link arms and smile at the NCB photographer in c.1979, after creating a new drift tunnel link with an existing roadway. The smaller image shows the actual heading machine used. 'Big-hitters' as they were sometimes known, the experienced men who created the new tunnels and drifts, were some of the top wage earners in the industry at this time. Kiveton was converted from a shaft mine to a drift mine in 1977 and further development took place from the mid 1980s. Although merging with High Moor Colliery in 1989, Kiveton's coal-life only lasted a few more years, production ending in 1994. *NCB*

THE CUTTER

Visit 'Woodhorn' virtually (www.experiencewoodhorn.com) or preferably in reality, the home of Woodhorn Museum and Northumberland Archives at Ashington and you will see and experience a modern building inspired by the great coal-cutters. The serrated roof of the building is a most spectacular feature, created by award-winning architect Tony Kettle and RMJM Scotland Ltd.

This spectacular image shows shaft-sinking taking place in relatively modern times, at the developing Redbrook Colliery, near Barnsley in 1982. Note the large sinking bucket or 'hoppit' used for the descent/ascent of men and materials. The completed shaft was used for ventilation. Redbrook was merged with its 'mother' pit Dodworth Colliery, the latter in effect closing, becoming part of the West Side Complex based around Woolley Colliery. All the expenditure and logistics did not result in longevity, Redbrook closing when Woolley closed, in 1987.

Four miners/sinking engineers are lowered in the hoppit during the excavation of the new shaft at Redbrook Colliery near Barnsley, an image evocative of pit-sinking operations generations earlier.

BEST FACE TONNAGE
K25's 42,474

BEST WEEKLY TONNAGE
61,000

Silverwood Colliery, near Rotherham, produced a million tons of coal during the 1985-86 financial year for the NCB, a remarkable achievement as it was just one year after the 1984-85 strike. The workforce then numbered 1342 and the Swallow Wood Seam was exploited using high-technology mining. Successes continued into the British Coal era as can be seen in this underground photograph. However, despite successes of the 80s and early 90s, coal production at Silverwood ended at the end of 1994.

'Roof-bolting' was one of the newer methods of supporting roof support in modern mines. Initially viewed with some concern by some miners and mine inspectors, it involved the upward drilling of holes into which bolts are inserted and anchored into the roof. Bars, girders, plates etc were also attached and secured, but was adopted fairly widely. In this way several roof beds could be linked together with no apparent hindrance of vertical supports. Here, in 1988, Stuart Woodlock of Exchem Mining and Construction can be seen demonstrating the bolting process watched by overman Stuart Beaumont at Houghton Main Colliery, near Barnsley. Stuart was in demand as a roof-bolt expert until his retirement in 2003. *Stuart Woodlock*

Britain's last coalfield, the so-called 'Selby Complex' in North Yorkshire failed to live up to its optimistic expectations despite the great efforts of hundreds of miners, many of whom had 'transferred' from closed collieries. In 1993, when in full production its 'superpit' achieved 110 million tonnes but by 2000 this annual figure had slumped to less than 5 million. Exchem roof-bolt man Stuart Woodlock (extreme left), and Whitemoor Mine's George Bond and Dave Armitage (surveyor) are pictured in the deep mine, one of the six main pits of Selby, on 23 May 1989. In an attempt to rationalise, if not salvage some production potential, Whitemoor was merged with Riccall – but mining ended here in 2004, and the great Selby dream was over. *Stuart Woodlock*

Chapter Five

Lock-outs and Strikes

An engraving showing the inside of a miner's cottage in Merthyr Tydfil was featured on the front page of the *Illustrated London News* of 18 January 1873. A woman is shown working the 'dolly-tub', washing clothes, the miner symbolically holding a pick alongside another woman and two young children. Seventy thousand south Wales miners had just gone on strike and were locked out of their pits following a 10 per cent reduction in wages.

The 1873 dispute in south Wales lasted almost three months, the miners returning to work on reduced pay. Towards the end of the dispute, the 15 February edition of the *Illustrated London News* emphasised the misery on its front page, women 'gathering shingles' to burn in their cottages. Following another even longer and unsuccessful strike in 1875 the South Wales and Monmouthshire Coal Owners' Association was formed. In effect this amalgamation curtailed effective protests of the miners for almost a generation. From now on the pitmen were paid via a 'sliding-scale' system, wage-rates dependant on the market price of coal. What was happening in Wales also occurred in various forms in other British coalfields. The 'coal-famine' period may have ended for domestic and commercial users but at a terrible cost to miners and their families. Outputs at pits increased as did manpower. There were 540,000 men and boys employed in the coal industry in 1875 but there were also 1,244 fatalities, 143 men and boys killed in a single disaster, at Swaithe Main, near Barnsley.

From Victorian times images showing 'soup kitchens' were routinely used in the media to demonstrate 'distress' in mining communities during strikes and lock-outs. This early example is a detail from an engraving featured on the front page of the *Illustrated London News* of 16 September 1893. The 'great lock-out' began on 30 July following a massive (25 per cent) reduction in wages.

At Acton Hall Colliery, Featherstone in West Yorkshire, on 7 September 1893, the Riot Act was read to 'striking' miners and their supporters. The troops that had been called in – a contingent of the First Battalion Staffordshire Regiment – following a warning volley, opened fire, killing two young men – James Gibbs (aged 21) and James Duggan (25) – and injuring several others. An artist's impression of the scene is the main image shown here. What became regarded in a pamphlet and the press as the 'Featherstone Massacre' left a tremendous amount of bad feeling towards the coal owners and authorities. The action of the troops was illegal and unnecessary, resulting in the deaths of two bystanders. This bitter national dispute ended two months later, a new Board of Conciliation now able to fix wage rates. The miners returned to work at the old, pre-strike rate of pay.

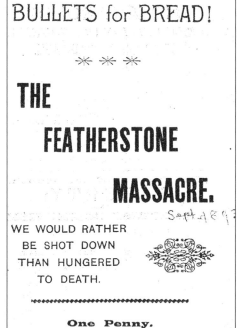

BULLETS for BREAD!

✳ ✳ ✳

THE

FEATHERSTONE

MASSACRE.

Sept. 1 8 9 3

WE WOULD RATHER
BE SHOT DOWN
THAN HUNGERED
TO DEATH.

One Penny.

In January 1903 720 miners and their families were evicted from company-owned properties by the Denaby and Cadeby colliery company during a 'bag-muck' strike over payment for the dirt that the miners extracted in the course of their 'hand-got' work. In a bitter winter of discontent families had to live in tents, chapels and schoolrooms, surviving on strike pay from the Yorkshire Miners' Association (YMA) and the goodwill of local people. The dispute continued until 22 March 1903. In a legal battle lasting until 1906 the YMA won its case against the coal owner. Two artists' interpretations capture the scene: an eviction in progress (notice the police involvement) and women and children being given a daily meal, cooked on chapel stove.

Also in Yorkshire, and not long after the Denaby evictions, about sixty families were ejected from their colliery-owned homes at Kinsley, near Fitzwilliam between August and October 2005. The process, which attracted widespread national interest, followed a long standing 'pay-reductions' dispute at Hemsworth-Fitzwilliam colliery. Initially a miners' camp was established, a canvas-clad tented community which was great copy for the media and a curiosity for sight-seers, but not very pleasant for the families. A small number of children were found temporary respite in the homes of several Barrow families, a situation that must have caused distress anyway; other youngsters benefitted from a stay at a local hotel. Offers of help came from far and wide, including Derbyshire, Lancashire and Cheshire. The dispute dragged on for 188 weeks, families surviving through donations and collections ('nipsey' money, so-called) and assistance from the new Miners' Federation of Great Britain. The men went back in June 1909, with even worse pay than what was offered before. The entire eviction process was well recorded by a series of contemporary picture postcards. In this image 'spectators' look towards the camera of Mr Wales of Hemsworth whilst bedding wrapped around personal effects is lowered from a bedroom window, several police officers facilitating the removal. One local apparently filled a trunk with bricks in order to gain amusement from the prospect and sight of the police struggling to lift the load. *Chris Sharp/Old Barnsley*

A small group of miners – possibly officials, based on their appearance and manner – outside a south Wales colliery during a 'coal strike' in 1910. This image could refer to the so-called 'Block Strike' of Aberdare rather than the more famous Cambrian Combine disturbances in the Rhondda. The dispute arose over the ending of a custom whereby miners were permitted to take home blocks of waste timber for use as household fuel; but widened to include a rightful demand that fair payment should be made for men working in difficult seams. The pit in the background may be Aberaman Colliery in the Cynon Valley, owned by the Powell Duffryn Company. Whatever the authenticity, this postcard provides us with a compelling image. The men face the photographer in a semi-formal pose, displaying a pick, shovel and lamp; and each man is smoking a pipe or cigarette, all of course wearing cloth caps. The formidable presence of the dog is perhaps understandable given the feelings at the time. The Aberdare dispute has received far less media attention than the riots at Tonypandy but in most respects was just as radical and alarming for the authorities to deal with, and just as painful for the strikers and their families. The Powell Duffryn miners returned to work on 2 January 1911 and received little benefit for their great efforts.

One of numerous 'strike scene' postcards issued for the Cambrian Combine dispute of 1910. A contingent of imported police and troops from Lancashire Fusiliers and the West Riding (of Yorkshire) Regiment assemble around a hoppit or sinking bucket at a pit head. The strike, which started with the lock-out at Ely Pit on 1 August 1910, dragged on for over a year and gained most media attention following the mass disturbances and miners-police clashes at Llwynypia Colliery and Tonypandy on 7-8 November. Winston Churchill's controversial decision – after some hesitation – to approve the deployment of troops left deep and lasting ill-feeling from Rhondda communities, the South Wales Miners' Federation in particular and the fast-developing labour movement as a whole. The miners went back defeated in terms of the fair pay that they wanted but demonstrated in no uncertain terms that they were prepared to stand up for their rights long-term, despite all the odds against them.

This wonderful social history photograph is typical of scenes in the coalfields of Britain during the strike of 1912. In this instance a group of miners and their families face the camera at an outcropping site at Lundhill Row, Wombwell, near Barnsley, the chimneys of Cortonwood Colliery visible in the upper left of the image. Just look at the expressions, especially on the children's faces, reflecting very hard times. The 'minimum wage' strike lasted from late February to mid-April and involved over a million miners.

Although a new Act of Parliament enforced a minimum wage and the men went back to work, coal owners were still able to combat national pay rates, which was why significant numbers of miners remained unhappy at the outcome, many of them preferring the dispute to continue. What had been clearly demonstrated, however, was that the miners were a formidable force to be reckoned with by governments, and now capable of launching and sustaining industrial action on a national scale. *Chris Sharp/Old Barnsley*

This unusual scene at a Wakefield (West Yorkshire area) pit was repeated elsewhere in various guises at many English collieries but especially in Yorkshire and Derbyshire during the 'striking summer' of 1919. Around 2.4 million workers had gone on strike, including, for a while, the police. The government was forced to call upon demobilised naval ratings to ensure that production continued at many collieries and to counteract what were thought to be Bolshevik-inspired activities in the aftermath of the Russian Revolution. Red-alert on one side, humour prevailed according to this representation. Note the tongue-in-cheek notices displayed on this occasion: 'A Happy Time at Ryhill Colliery' and 'Good Old Yorkshire Pudding'. *Chris Sharp/Old Barnsley*

Hard times. During the 1921 coal strike miners in many areas, as they did at other times, open up levels or drifts in hillsides in order to access shallow seams of coal and keep their home fires burning. This is an interesting example, from Llwynypia in the Rhondda, the miner with a pick over his shoulder wearing a ball and peg lamp on his cap. Notice also the simple but effective pulley system that they had installed, with a bag of coal hoisted for display, perhaps to be placed on a push-bike, barrow or cart for distribution. The young lad on the extreme right sitting next to the ball and peg man hardly looks old enough to be working. *Stewart Williams Publisher*

The miners' 'lock-out' following the 1926 General Strike resulted in a great deal of distress for families already suffering poverty in the coalfields of Britain and postcard publishers demonstrated this in 'soup kitchen' images. These typical examples show staff and helpers from Newtongrange, Midlothian, Scotland (upper image) and the village of Gelli, Ystrad in the Rhondda Fawr area of south Wales (lower image). Newtongrange had become the largest pit village in Scotland following the development of Lady Victoria Colliery (now the Scottish Mining Museum). *Scottish Mining Museum/Stewart Williams Publisher*

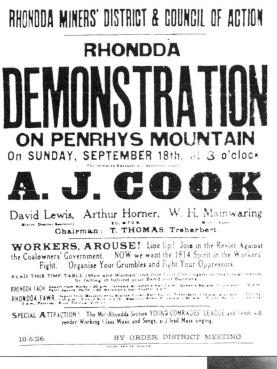

RHONDDA MINERS' DISTRICT & COUNCIL OF ACTION

RHONDDA

DEMONSTRATION

ON PENRHYS MOUNTAIN

On SUNDAY, SEPTEMBER 18th, at 3 o'clock

The following Speakers will positively attend:

A. J. COOK

David Lewis, Arthur Horner, W. H. Mainwaring

Chairman: T. THOMAS, Treherbert.

WORKERS, AROUSE! Line Up! Join in the Revolt Against the Coalowners' Government. NOW we want the 1914 Spirit in the Workers' Fight. Organise Your Grumbles and Fight Your Oppressors.

READ THIS TIME TABLE (Men and Women) and Join Your Contingent in this Great March, by falling in behind your Band and Banners.

RHONDDA FACH: Depart from Maerdy 1.30 p.m. Carnegie Workmen's Hall 2 p.m. Queen's Square Tylorstown 3.0 p.m. Ferndale Square Maerdy, 1.30 Workmen's Hall Ystrad 2 p.m.

RHONDDA FAWR: Depart from Blaenrhondda Station 1 p.m. Workmen's Hall Square Treherbert 1.15 p.m. Pandy Square, Treorchy 2 p.m. Penrhiwfer, Royal Theatre 2.15 p.m.

SPECIAL ATTRACTION! The Mid-Rhondda Section YOUNG COMRADES' LEAGUE and Bands will render Working Class Music and Songs, and Lead Mass singing.

18.5/26.   BY ORDER DISTRICT MEETING.

The miners' leader A.J. Cook was a key and charismatic figure during the 6-month 'lock-out' of 1926. As a boy he worked as farm labourer in Somerset, moving to Trefor Colliery in the Rhondda in 1901, aged 17. By 1924 Cook was Secretary of 800,000-strong Miners' Federation of Great Britain and his passionate and eloquent campaign for miners' rights was encapsulated in what became one of the most famous of all working-class quotes: 'Not a minute on the day, not a penny off the pay'. Cook hurt his leg in a scuffle at a public meeting in 1926, amputation having to follow, and he eventually died of cancer on 2 November 1931, at the relatively young age of 46. Here he can be seen making a point at a 'peace rally' in Trafalgar Square London and the poster, on display along with a Tussaud-style model of himself, is on view in the Rhondda Heritage Park's visitor centre.

On 26 June 1937 the president of the Harworth branch of the Nottingham Miners' Association Mick Cane was given 2 years with hard labour for 'inciting a riot', by far the most severe of the sentences imposed on ten other Nottinghamshire union men (and one miner's wife) following a longstanding dispute. Five others of the so-called 'Seventeen' on trial were bound over. The sentences resulted in widespread condemnation from the labour movement. Kane, seen here with his niece, baby Pat, after his release in August 1937. The breakaway and 'non-political' Nottinghamshire and District Miners' Union founded by George Spencer was merged with the NMA in 1937, Spencer becoming the new President.

Wives and children of Staffordshire miners warm themselves outside the open fire in the cold and rain outside Rugely Power Station on 18 January 1972. The women can be seen reading copies of the latest edition of the NUM newspaper *The Miner* and children hold home-made placards with messages of protest displayed, such as MY DADDY SHOULD HAVE A LIVING WAGE...GIVE US A FAIR WAGE. The miners' picket 'camp' is just visible in the background. The dispute over pay had begun on 9 January and was the first national strike since 1926. Initially picketing was confined to coal-fired stations but was soon widened so as to include all power stations and 'strategic targets' such as steelworks, ports and coal depots. There were in fact two stations at Rugely, Station A commissioned in 1956 and Rugely B opened in 1970, taking coal by conveyor belt from neighbouring Lea Hall Colliery. Although the pit closed in 1991 station B continues to function as Rugely Power Limited.

Power stations well outside coalfield areas were picketed in 1972, attracting a good deal of media attention. This somewhat staged example, at Battersea, near London took place on 2 February. Roy Mason, MP for Barnsley, himself a former miner (and Minister of Power) is seen (pipe in mouth) warming his hands over a battered brazier. The two pickets sitting near him are Hedley Crewe (centre) and Grant Few (aged 17) from Betteshanger, Kent's biggest pit. Mason was among fifteen NUM-sponsored MPs who joined striking miners on the picket line. Battersea had its coal delivered from ports in south Wales and North East England. It was decommissioned in 1983 and remains the largest brick building in Europe, though 'at risk' according to English Heritage. It now forms part of a private residential development project. Betteshanger is believed to have been the only pit that went on strike during the Second World War. It closed in 1989. *Mason Archive*

The saddest day of the 1972 strike occurred on 4 February when a young Hatfield Main miner, Freddie Matthews, lost his life after being crushed by the rear of an articulated lorry when picketing at Keadby Power Station in Lincolnshire. Around 10,000 miners and supporters attended Fred's funeral a few days later, as can be seen in this compelling image. Nationally, a state of emergency was declared by the Heath government and a 3-day week was introduced in order to save energy.

Picketing was widespread during the 1972 strike but it was the organised and strategic use of 'flying pickets' and then 'mass picketing' at the Saltley Coke Works, Birmingham that attracted so much media attention and remains in the memory. The closure of the works was seen as a great victory for the miners and gave confidence for further and future actions. The Wilberforce Inquiry included what was regarded as substantial pay rises, placing miners near the top of industrial workers' wages. However, there were inherent clauses concerning productivity and a 16-month timescale, as well as other niggles. After initially rejecting Wilberforce, the NUM executive recommended balloting members. Thus on 25 February there was an overwhelming acceptance, and a return to work three days later. The 7-week winter strike was over. Not long afterwards, a Woolley Colliery delegate, one of the main strategists of the Yorkshire picketing teams and the Saltley campaign in particular was elected full-time compensation agent for the Yorkshire Area, and was elected as its president in 1973. His name was Arthur Scargill.

Rescue workers examine mine plans at Lofthouse Colliery near Wakefield on 23 March 1973, perhaps hoping against hope that any of the lost men would have found an air pocket and survived. Two days earlier there was a great inrush of water when face development workers accidentally broke into an abandoned mineshaft which had been flooded for many years. Despite all efforts, including the use of specialist teams of underwater divers, only one body was recovered, sadly deceased, that of Charles Cotton. Six other miners were never found. More than 40 years later, Tony Banks, a 71 year old survivor of the disaster, refuses to forget his late friends and continues to lead commemorations. The Lofthouse tragedy attracted national and international media coverage. Arthur Scargill represented the Yorkshire Area NUM on site and took part in some of the search operations; and led questioning during the subsequent public inquiry.

On 24 January 1974 miners voted overwhelmingly in favour of strike action following an NEC-recommended ballot. The 'Yes-vote' was convincing: 81% on average and over 90% in the south Wales and Yorkshire areas. Since Wilberforce miners' wages had plummeted to 18th in the industrial pay league. An overtime ban had been in force for several weeks. The Heath government's implementation of a three-day week and state of emergency proved to be a dangerous strategy, politically and economically. The strike started on 9 February.

Picketing during the 1974 miners' strike was much more restrained in the wake of the recently imposed Industrial Relations Act but, in February, with their makeshift shelter and wood-fired brazier this small group of miners at Birley East pit, near Sheffield manage to keep warm and cheerful. Following the 'who rules Britain' general election at the end of the month, the return of a Labour government and a Pay Board report, the miners returned to work. Two 'non-pay' but very important aspects of the settlement concerned the implementation of new arrangements for pneumoconiosis claims and a superannuation scheme. *Sheffield Star*

With his long sideburns and teddy boy-style outfit, Brian Hibbard was the distinctive lead vocalist of a cappello group called The Flying Pickets. Ebbw Vale-born, from a socialist background, Hibbard had joined the theatre company '7:84' (7% of the population control 84% of the wealth), touring *One Big Blow*, about a miners' brass band. Forming The Flying Pickets was apt as the group actively supported the miners and their strikes; and were able to do so in a high profile manner after the great success of their first single *Only You*, a Christmas No.1 in 1983. Virgin, their record company were unhappy at their associations with the miners and WH Smith even refused to stock their records, but *When You're Young and in Love* (1984) was another hit that furthered their popularity. After Brian Hibbard left TFP in 1986 he continued working as a soap and character actor until his death from prostate cancer in 2012, and is sadly missed. The modern image is of Brian outside the picket caravan at the Big Pit mining museum, Blaenafon in 2008. TFP, though now without any original members, continue to record and tour. *Big Pit (Amgueddfa Cymru/National Museum Wales)*

A rare view showing the inside of what became the famous picket 'hut' of 'The Alamo' at the head of the pit lane leading to Cortonwood Colliery at Brampton in South Yorkshire during the 1984 strike. It was the pit manager's unofficial announcement that Cortonwood was to close, made to a passing local NUM branch secretary, through the wound-down side window of his car, that started the chain of events that began a year-long strike, generally regarded by social historians as the most significant industrial dispute in twentieth century British history. The Cortonwood miners had earlier been assured that the pit had five years further life, and a new face was already in development at considerable expense. State documents recently released from The National Archives under the 25-year rule confirm what has been known in coalfield communities for many years, that the Conservative Government of Margaret Thatcher was well-prepared to engage and defeat the miners and that the use of the police (and related security services) was integral to this strategy. There was to be no repeat of 1972 and especially 1974.

The rank and file miners and the women were the unsung heroes of the 1984-85 strike. Pictured here is Terrence Picken, still proud to show his allegiance to Cortonwood Colliery when interviewed in 2000. Terry (wearing a black wool cap in the previous photograph) was a regular picket at The Alamo, even after contracting pneumonia. Although his village, Brampton, was 'under siege' with police and media on occasions during 1984/85, picketing was generally peaceful and uneventful, as it was elsewhere. Not surprising that in The Alamo they played cards to pass the time. It was the more violent confrontations that were the focus of the media, often relayed as if it was the norm.

Wearing his 20-year-old 'strike cardigan', emblazoned with badges, veteran Yorkshire miner Arthur Wakefield never missed a day's picketing or fund raising during the 1984-85 strike. What is even more remarkable was the way he recorded his day-to-day experiences in a journal, written in longhand in old Woolworth's scrapbooks. The contents, alongside a selection of the many photographs that he took on a regular basis, were published as *The Miners' Strike Day by Day* in 2002.

Arthur Wakefield recorded many scenes and incidents during his very active year on strike, armed with nothing more than a cheap camera. His snapshots may lack the technical and artistic standards of the professional photographers of the time but they represent a very honest attempt by a participant and eyewitness and as such will remain important social records for many years to come. These two examples relate to Orgreave coking plant near Sheffield on 18 June 1984, the first in the relative calm and the second in the aftermath of numerous 'cavalry' and police dog charges. Later this day became known via the media as 'The Battle of/for Orgreave'. In the wake of the Hillsborough report of 2012 the Independent Police Complaints Commission began a 'scoping' exercise in order to ascertain if there is a case for a full investigation into the events and aftermath of 18 June but at the time of writing, after more than 20 months nothing has appeared.

There were several outstanding professional photographers who covered the great miners' strike and one of the best was Peter Arkell, who worked for News Line in 1984 (and freelance from 1985). Here, at the mass May-day rally at Mansfield Peter, from a sea of strikers, picks out a lone, arguably symbolic home-made placard from the Clipstone contingent, which says: UNITY WILL WIN... THE SCABS WILL LOSE. The striking miners in Nottinghamshire were in the minority, by far, most Notts men preferring to continue working in the absence of a ballot or even joining a new union: The Union of Democratic Miners (UDM), formed in December 1984. *Peter Arkell*

This dramatic image captured by Peter Arkell shows police using force to arrest a striking miner during lobbying outside Parliament during the 1984-85 strike, the majority of the crowd restrained behind barricades. *Peter Arkell*

Perhaps the most outstanding and most positive feature of the 84-85 miners' strike concerned the role of women, so many groups emerging in support, raising funds and organising food distribution. Without the likes of Binny Jones from Blaenau Ffestiniog, who smiles to the photographer as she carries a box of donated food, there would have been little or no community spirit. *Amgueddfa Cymru/National Museum Wales*

Women were also active on the picket lines, especially in or near to their own communities. Here, the Ladies' section of Clipstone Colliery pause for a photograph on their way back from a picket line. They are, left to right: Margaret Anderson, Carol Potter, Jane Holness and Elsie Lowe. *Jonathan Symcox*

The Rhymney Valley (South Wales) Women's Support Group lead the 'march back to work' at the end of the strike, in March 1985. The last of the Valley's deep mines, Penallta, closed in 1991. Elliot Colliery's winding house is now the centre-piece of the Winding House Museum at New Tredegar. *Amgueddfa Cymru/National Museum Wales*

This in many ways extraordinary photograph, taken on 2 July 1985, is of Prime Minister Margaret Thatcher opening the annual art exhibition of works by MPs and peers in the House of Commons. Roy Mason, the MP for Barnsley Central (and a former mineworker) can be seen pointing to his entry, which has the theme of LEST WE FORGET, featuring a montage of images relating to the very recent miners' strike. Mrs Thatcher's customary attentiveness is tempered with concern as she views some of the images featuring herself. *Mason Archive*

Anne Scargill (centre) and other veteran members of the Women Against Pit Closure movement pictured at a miners' gala at Denaby Main in 2009. The lady on the extreme left is Lesley Boulton who was the subject of what became John Harris's famous photograph showing a mounted police officer raising his baton to strike her on the head – at Orgreave, on the hot sunny day of 18 June 1984. Lesley had been peacefully taking photographs and was attending to an injured miner; and was just wanting to attract attention when the charge took place. Fortunately she managed to avoid the strike and what could have been a serious personal injury. Betty Cook is on the extreme right, holding a miner's lamp.

Have a Nice Day... John Harris's subsequently famous photograph of a mounted police officer attempting to strike a female bystander at Orgreave was parodied by cartoonist Frank (aka Francis) Boyle for the *Labour Weekly* newspaper; and sums up very well the mood of the times. Information about Frank and his work can be accessed via www.boylecartoon.co.uk   *Frank Boyle*

Chapter Six

Mining Miscellany

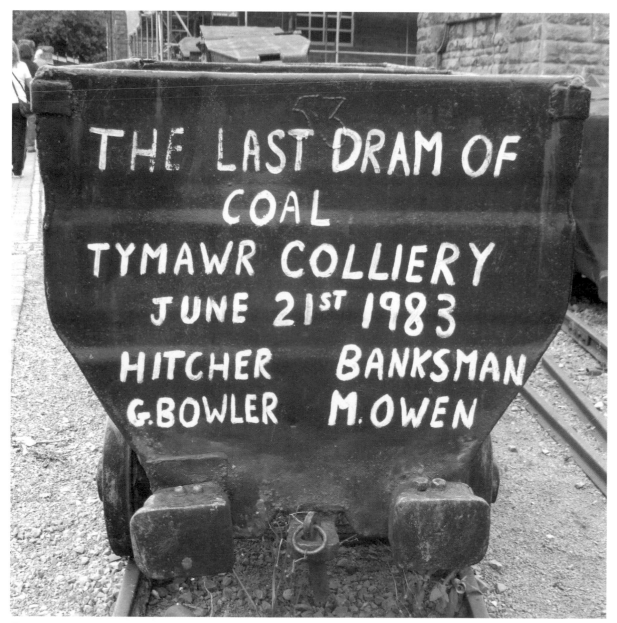

This exhibit can be seen at the Rhondda Heritage Centre.

A deputy or fireman carefully inspects the flame of his lamp, his cap lamp providing the directed illumination. The lamp is held high, close to the roof, where methane might accumulate. When gas was present the flame diminished in proportion to the volume of the gas. If the methane or firedamp as it was known exploded the resultant 'afterdamp' (carbon monoxide) was usually the cause of most fatalities. This posed image, by the photographer W. Suschitzky, dates from about 1950 and is believed to have been taken underground at Ellington Colliery, Northumberland. 'Big "E"', sunk by the Ashington Coal Company in 1909, employed more than 2,000 persons in the 1980s, but was closed by its last owners, UK Coal, in 2005, the last deep mine in the North East of England.
W.Suschitzky

A former miner at the Snibston Discovery Museum (www.snibston.com), Coalville, Leicestershire, demonstrates one of the earliest – and most dangerous – forms of lighting in coal mines: the candle. The site includes the former Snibston Colliery and there are guided tours and a variety of events.

A Victorian 'Davy-style' gauzed-encased flame safety lamp is demonstrated at the Rhondda Heritage Park on the site of Lewis Merthyr Colliery, Trehafod (www.rhonddaheritagepark.com) where visitors can access an Underground Experience Tour and 'live the experience' of the life of a miner.

After the Russian Revolution and Great World War many miners' banners featured images of Marx and Lenin. This fine Chopwell Lodge (Durham) example also included the Labour pioneer James Keir Hardie, who had worked in the Scottish mines as a boy 'trapper' (opening and closing underground safety doors). Hardie served as MP for West Ham South (1892-5) and, most famously for Merthyr Tydfil (1900-15). Chopwell closed in 1966.

First organised and held by the Durham Miners' association in 1871, the 'Big Meeting' as it became known continues to attract more than 100,000 people every year. At the end of the Second World War there were over 100 collieries and 112,000 miners in Durham but by 1993, in the wake of the pit closures following the 1984-85 strike none remained. But this great tradition of working-class culture continues and long may it do so. Here, the Thornley Colliery banner takes pride of place in 2012. Thornley was sunk in 1835 but suffered an early disaster when seven miners lost their lives in an explosion, the fatalities including a boy trapper aged only nine years and two 11-year-olds. This old pit employed over a thousand men during the 1960s, closing in 1970. *GMB (trade union)*

The town of Barnsley has a proud tradition of hosting Yorkshire miners' galas and demonstrations. The Grimethorpe Colliery banner can be seen here leading the march down Market Hill in 1969 on the way to Locke Park where the speeches and entertainment was held, attracting thousands of people. The speakers included the local MP (and Minister of Fuel and Power) Roy Mason and the well-known Scottish miners' leader and new NUM General Secretary Lawrence Daley. Notice the children 'riding the banner', always a popular sight at galas, and the large number of spectators lining the route. But the smartly-dressed veteran miner in the foreground, holding one of the rope guides attached to the upper part of the banner structure, really makes the picture for me: he was clearly proud to be there. *NUM (Yorks)*

In recent years, the historic and cultural importance of colliery banners has been much appreciated, especially at commemorative and celebratory events. The oldest surviving examples, usually silk-based, are far too fragile for public marches and 'unprotected' public access, needing conservation and then museum conditions for storage and display. There were often 'generations of banners' for single collieries or lodges, new ones replacing old 'worn-out' or damaged versions. The excellent South Wales Miners' Library, part of the Swansea University's South Wales Coalfield Collection, located on the Hendrefoelan Campus (swansea.ac.uk/iss/swm) has a special interest in miners' banners and holds 39 examples. This relatively modern Newland Lodge banner, dating from c.1964 can be seen on display there. It features two working miners and Will Paynter, the well-known miners' leader famous as a young man for his participation in the hunger marches of the 1930s and his involvement as a volunteer in the Spanish Civil War. President of the South Wales NUM from 1951, Paynter also served as General Secretary of the NUM from 1959 to 1968, succeeded by Lawrence Daly. The images are set above a 'Lest We Forget' legend. Newland Colliery, one of the smaller Welsh mines, worked coal under Margram Bay, from about the end of the Great War, closing in 1968.

This rare image is of a small group of miners at Birchenwood (formerly Kidsgrove) Colliery, Staffordshire. By their appearance, their lamps and sticks, they are probably senior officials, engineers and managers. A well-publicised royal visit took place here on 22 April 1913, so the photograph may well relate to the occasion when George V and Queen Mary came to the colliery. The royal party, 'regulars' when it came to visiting mines, saw the new German-designed coke ovens, at one of the largest byproduct plants in the country, using state-of-the art technology. The colliery closed c.1932 but coke and other byproducts continued to be produced here until 1973.

HM Queen Elizabeth II is seen leaving the cage which brought her up from an underground tour of Rothes Pit, Kirkaldy, Fifeshire, on 30 June 1958, after officially opening the colliery. It was said to be her first visit descent of a coal mine. The young Queen was kitted out with a white boiler suit, with matching headscarf and helmet. Her guide, probably the colliery manager, can be seen carrying a new miner's lamp, which was probably presented to her as part of the occasion. The Queen was accompanied by the Duke of Edinburgh on the surface and underground. Rothes had actually started production a year earlier, in 1957, and was hailed by the NCB as a 'superpit'. Geological problems and severe flooding led to the closure of Rothes after only five years – and considerable embarrassment for the NCB, its consultants and the Government after c.£20 million (equal to about £436.5 million today) of taxpayers' money had been spent on the project. A new town, Glenrothes, was built in anticipation that the pit had a predicted life of a hundred years.

A team of official photographers were employed by the NCB, many of their images used in *Coal News* and for media distribution. Jeff Poar, seen here following an underground 'shift' at Kellingley Colliery in c.1982, had an office in Coal House, Doncaster. Jeff came from a mining background, his father and brothers from Hirwain, Rhondda Cynon Taff, south Wales. Jeff got his dream job as a photographer after working in another unusual role for the NCB, as a chauffeur, driving Coal Board VIPs. He took some superb photographs of miners in a variety of settings and put down the quality of his pictures to having an instant relationship with the miners rather than in technical equipment and knowhow. Jeff was given little notice to 'clear his desk' after being made redundant in the aftermath of the 1984-85 strike but I was fortunate to record some of his memories, now deposited at the National Coal Mining Museum for England and in the Discovery Centre (Archives) of the new Experience Barnsley museum. *Jeff Poar*

Will (John William) Streets was born at Whitwell in Derbyshire on 24 March 1886, the eldest of twelve children. As a teenager he worked underground at the local colliery, driving ponies by the age of 15 according to the 1901 census and hewing coal – as did his father – ten years later. Though academically talented and interested in writing, he must have needed to work to help support such a large family. After the start of the First World War in 1914 Will enlisted, joining the 12th Service Battalion of the York and Lancaster Regiment (the Sheffield Pals). By April 1916 he was on the Somme battlefield, at Serre, and when the great offensive started on 1 July he was a Sergeant, therefore led a group of soldiers. Will was wounded but returned to attend to another casualty but then disappeared, feared dead, aged 31. His body was discovered and identified ten months later, on 1 May 1917. Will's personal effects included letters, diaries and two books of poems. William John Streets's headstone can be seen at the Euston Road Cemetery, Colincamps. We have a glimpse of why Streets wrote his poems in a surviving letter sent to a publisher, which includes the following:

'I have tried to picture some thoughts that pass through a man's brain when he dies. I may not see the end of the poems, but I hope to live to do so. We soldiers have our views of life to express, though the boom of death is in our ears.'

Streets's literary ambition was never fulfilled in his short life but in 1924 a collection of his poems appeared in print under the title of *The Undying Splendour*. Far less well-known than the likes of Wilfred Owen or Siegfried Sassoon, this former Derbyshire miner deserves to be remembered.

Many miners serving in the Great War were awarded gallantry medals but 'Jack' (John) Henry Williams, a Company Sergeant in the 10th Battalion South Wales Borderers, was one of the most decorated of them all. For 'conspicuous gallantry action' during the capture of Mametz Wood on 10-12 July 1916 he received the DCM (Distinguished Conduct Medal); then, just over a year later, on 31 July 1917, during the third battle of Ypres, his bravery was recognised in the form of an MM (Military Medal). A bar was added to his MM following his rescue, under fire, of a wounded colleague at Armentieres on 30 October of the same year. Towards the end of the war, on the night of 7-8 October 1918, during an attack on Villers Outreaux, Williams, again under heavy fire, charged an enemy machine gun, bayonetting five (of fifteen) of his captives when they rebelled. For this extraordinary act of bravery he was awarded the Victoria Cross (VC). Severely wounded by shrapnel, the former colliery blacksmith from Cwm village was discharged from the army on medical grounds a few days later. He was subsequently decorated with the Medaille Militaire by the French and at Buckingham Palace George V presented him, separately, with FOUR bravery awards, a unique occurrence. A commemorative plaque in honour of CSM J.H. Williams was unveiled at the General Offices building of the former Ebbw Vale Steel iron and Coal Company (now Gwent Archives) in 2014.

Visit Beamish open air museum (www.beamish.org.uk) and you can take an underground tour of the old Mahogany mine in the presence and guidance of a former miner dressed in Victorian-style work clothes. The drift, a 'walk-in' mine, dates from the 1850s and would have used small ponies to haul pubs of coal to the surface (and later by mechanised rope haulage). Mahogany closed in 1958 but was given a new lease of 'educational' life in 1979 when it was officially re-opened by Sir Derek Ezra. Sir Derek (now Lord) Ezra was then the well-regarded chairman of the NCB, a post he held from 1972 to 1982.

Publisher's note:
Also available from Pen & Sword is Brian Elliott's *Tracing Your Coalmining Ancestors* book. *Miners and the Great War* and *Mine Disasters and Mine Rescue* will be featured in forthcoming books by Brian as part of our military, mining heritage and *Images of the Past* series. Please check our website for further details, and for many other mine-related and family history books: www.pen-and-sword.co.uk